IN THE BEGINNING

IN THE
BEGINNING

A New Interpretation of Genesis

KAREN ARMSTRONG

ALFRED A. KNOPF · NEW YORK 1996

Grateful acknowledgment is made to the *National Council
of the Churches of Christ in the USA* for permission to
reprint scripture quotations from the *New Revised Standard
Version of the Bible,* copyright © 1989 by the Division
of Christian Education of the National Council of the
Churches of Christ in the USA. All rights reserved.
Reprinted by permission.

Library of Congress Cataloging-in-Publication Data
Armstrong, Karen.
In the beginning: a new interpretation of Genesis / by
Karen Armstrong. — 1st ed.
p.   cm.
Includes bibliographical references and index.
ISBN 0-679-45089-0 (alk. paper)
1.Bible. O.T. Genesis—Criticism, interpretation, etc. I. Title.
BS1235.2A76 1996
222'. 1106—dc20   96-26170   CIP

Manufactured in the United States of America
First Edition

For Kate Jones and John Tackaberry

Contents

Contents

A NEW
INTERPRETATION
OF GENESIS

Wrestling with God and Scripture

ONE OF THE MOST HAUNTING SCENES IN Genesis is surely the occasion when Jacob wrestled all night long with a mysterious stranger and discovered that he had in reality been struggling with God (Genesis 32:24–32). It was a moment of crisis. Jacob was returning to his homeland after an absence of twenty years. He feared that his brother, Esau, whom he had gravely wronged, would kill him when they met the next day. He was full of dread and felt inadequate for the task that God had set him. That night Jacob camped alone at the wild gorge of the Jabbok stream on the borders of Canaan. There, the biblical writer tells us laconically, "a man wrestled with him until daybreak." When he found that he could not overpower Jacob, his assailant struck him on the hip, dislocating it, just as the dawn was breaking. Still Jacob refused to let him go and, for once in his confused life, was able to rise superbly to the occasion. He knew that this was no ordinary opponent, yet he did not ask for a revelation or a miracle. Instead, he asked for a blessing and was given a new name: "You shall no longer be called Jacob," said the stranger, "but Israel, for you have striven with God and with humans, and have prevailed."

> Then Jacob asked him, "Please tell me your name." But he said, "Why is it that you ask my name?" And there he blessed him. So Jacob called the place Peniel, saying, "For I have seen God face to face, and yet my life is preserved." (32:29–30)

It is surprising to find this incident in the Hebrew Bible. Later the descendants of Jacob/Israel would insist that no human being could look upon the face of God and live. They would find it blasphemous to imagine their deity appearing to any mortal—however august—in human form. Yet the editors who put together the final text of Genesis in about the fifth century BCE felt able to include the tale because it so eloquently described the religious experience of Israel. There would be no final revelation: God would never fully impart his name and nature to his people. The sacred was too great a reality to be contained within a purely human definition or system of thought. Thus, the people of Israel would have only fleeting and frequently ambiguous glimpses of the divine, though they would know that they had been blessed. Their lives had been touched by a reality that transcended mundane existence, and that elusive contact gave them the strength and insight to face the challenge of an uncertain world. After this strange encounter with God, Jacob left Peniel, limping from his damaged hip, just as the sun was rising, fully prepared to face his brother and achieve the difficult reconciliation. Above all, the Israelites recognized the image of the wrestling match. They did not imagine their religious heroes achieving enlightenment effortlessly or with the calm serenity of a Buddha. Salvation was a painful, difficult process. Hence the significance of the very name "Israel," which can be translated "One who struggles with God" or even "God-fighter."

Jacob's mysterious combat at the Jabbok is also an emblem of the painful effort that the Bible so often demands of its readers. In almost all cultures, scripture has been one of the tools that men and women have used to apprehend a dimension that transcends their normal lives. People have turned to their holy books not to acquire information but to have an experience. They have encountered a reality there that goes beyond their normal existence but endows it with ultimate significance. They have given this transcendence different names—Brahman, dharma, nirvana, or God—but, however we choose to describe or interpret it, it has been a fact of human life. We are constantly aware of an ideal level that contrasts with the world around us. We may not regard this realm as supernatural; we may prefer to find it in art, music, or poetry rather than in a church or synagogue. But human beings have persistently sought a dimension of existence that seems close to our normal lives and yet far from them. Sacred scripture has been one of the principal means of introducing people to a world of ultimate truth, beauty, and goodness. It has helped human beings to cultivate a sense of the eternal and the absolute in the midst of the transient world in which they find themselves.

But we have to know how to read our scriptures. They demand an imaginative effort that can sometimes be as perplexing and painful as Jacob's wrestling match. The true meaning of scripture can never be wholly comprised in a literal reading of the text, since that text points beyond itself to a reality which cannot adequately be expressed in words and concepts. Hindus, for example, believe that the sound of the words in the Vedas is just as important as their lexical sense. Thus the syllable *om* has no conceptual significance, but when people have chanted it, listening to the silence that precedes and follows it, they feel that they have found a mysterious bridge to the divine. Buddhists of the Nichiren school have discovered that chanting the mere title of the Lotus Sutra yields access not only to the truths of the book but to the ineffable reality that lies beyond them. Many Buddhists and Muslims are able to derive inspiration from a scripture written in a language that they do not understand.

This is obviously very different from the way we normally read books in the modern West. Our scientific culture trains us to look for the literal truths of the words on the page. We expect a text to express its ideas as clearly as possible. In a philosophical or historical work, we will often judge writers by the precision and consistency of their arguments; we are likely to condemn a work that is deliberately vague or paradoxical or that presents mutually exclusive arguments. There are many Jews and Christians who have come to apply the same standards to the Bible. Some, for example, have argued that the first chapter of Genesis is a factual account of the beginning of life on earth: they believe that God really did make the world in six days, and that those scientists who maintain that it took billions of years to evolve must be wrong. What we need to understand is that the Bible does not present its truths to us in this way. Reading it demands the same kind of meditative and intuitive attention that we give to a poem. We often have to wrestle with the text, only to learn that we are denied the certainty of a final revelation.

Genesis has been one of the sacred books that have enabled millions of men and women to know at some profound level that human life has an eternal dimension, even though they have not always been able to express this insight in logical, rational form. Like any scripture, Genesis points to a reality that must essentially transcend it. But the writers employ different methods from those of the Hindu Vedas or the Buddhist Sutras. The biblical authors force us to make an imaginative effort. They imply that it is a hard struggle to discern a sacred reality in the flawed and tragic conditions in which we live and that our experience will often be disconcerting or contradictory. Like Jacob, we will have to wrestle in the dark, denied the consolations of final certitude and experiencing at best only transient, elusive blessing. We may even find that we have been wounded in the course of our struggle.

Beginnings

AS ITS NAME IMPLIES, GENESIS TRACES THE early stages of the human relationship with the divine. It is a story of beginnings: the beginning of the world, of the human race, of the people of Israel, and of our experience of the reality that we call "God." As a story of beginnings, it is full of pain, confusion, and false starts. It speaks of the difficulty of human generation, of the pangs of childbirth and the anguish of the family life which introduces us all into the world. But like any scripture, Genesis has been treasured not for the light it throws on the irretrievably distant past but for its timeless relevance to the present. The authors of Genesis do not give us historical information about life in Palestine during the second millennium BCE. In fact, as scholars have shown, they knew nothing about the period. Frequently they made mistakes, referring to the presence of the Philistines, for example, who did not arrive in the country until long after this early biblical era. They speak of towns, such as Beersheva, which did not yet exist. They make no mention of the strong Egyptian presence in Palestine at this time. Our authors are not interested in historical accuracy, however. Instead they bring to the reader's attention important truths about the human predicament that still reverberate today. So much is this the case that, while writing this essay and recounting some of these stories, I continually found myself using the present tense and had to make a conscious effort to relegate the events I was describing to the past. It seemed, for example, more natural to say that Jacob *fights* with his mysterious assailant and *pleads* for a blessing. It is not merely that these stories, learned in early childhood, are a familiar part of our imaginative world and are, therefore, in some sense continuously present to us. They have an emblematic, archetypal quality that, for instance, makes Jacob's struggle our own. The author is not simply describing an incident in the life of the patriarch but revealing a mysterious dynamic in the human psyche, and this means that his story speaks as immediately to a reader today as it did in his own time.

The tales of Genesis have a timeless quality because they address those regions of the spirit that remain opaque to us and yet exert an irresistible fascination. A reading of Genesis suggests how it was that psychoanalysis began as a predominantly Jewish discipline. Long before Freud, the authors of ancient Israel had already begun to explore the uncharted realm of the human mind and heart. They saw this struggle with the emotions and with the past as the theater of the religious quest. By seeking reconciliation with the people who have damaged them in the past and by attempting to resolve their inner conflicts, men and women would sense that harmony and peace which characterize the sacred. Yet precisely because the authors of Genesis are dealing with such fundamental and difficult matters, they give us few precise teachings. There are no glib or facile messages in Genesis. It is impossible to find a clear theology in its pages; the authors share no moral consensus, and some have ethics which we would find highly dubious today. There are no paragons in these tales, and even God's behavior occasionally leaves something to be desired. Even though Genesis has played so significant a role in shaping the Judeo-Christian tradition, the book can often challenge our religious preconceptions and shows that, like all human reflections on the divine, it cannot adequately express the frequently baffling reality to which it directs our attention.

Creation

 YET WHEN WE TURN TO THE FIRST CHAPTER of Genesis, which describes the creation of the universe, it seems to be providing us with exactly the sort of God and worldview that conventional religion teaches us to expect. We find a single God in center stage, the sole source of power and life, totally in control of his creation. God is isolated and unique, entirely distinct from the natural world, which is wholly subordinate to him. God has simply to speak and his words articulate the formless waste of chaos, giving it grammar, shape, and form:

> Then God said, "Let there be light"; and there was light. And God saw that the light was good; and God separated the light from the darkness. God called light Day, and the darkness he called Night. And there was evening and there was morning, the first day. (Genesis 1:3–5)

This masterly account, written by a member of the Priestly school (and therefore known by scholars as P) in the sixth century BCE, emphasizes the purposefulness of God's creativity. This deity does not, in Einstein's famous phrase, play dice. Key words are repeated throughout the chapter. God "said," "saw," "separated," and "called." The stately rhythm and repetition make us feel that events are following a serenely ordained pattern. Similarly, God's pronouncement that each stage of his creation is "good" emphasizes the excellence, rightness, and wholesomeness of the universe. This God is not only powerful but completely benevolent. The structure of the text rises to a crescendo: the author devotes more time and space to each successive day. Finally everything converges on the sixth day, when humanity is created, and God pronounces his world "very good" (1–31).

There seem to be no surprises in the Priestly account of creation, therefore. This is the omnipotent, transcendent, and benevolent God of classical theism. The world that he created has pattern and meaning. It is also hierarchically arranged, with God at the apex of the pyramid and human beings as his deputies on earth, granted "dominion over the fish of the sea, and over the birds of the air, and over the cattle, and over all the wild animals of the earth, and over every creeping thing that creeps upon the earth" (1:26). The repeated motif of separation—of light from darkness, sea from dry land, day from night—shows that this is a world where boundaries are important. Plants, animals, and fish are all classified according to their species. Everything must keep to the place allotted to it and must not transgress its limits. The text seems to support the conventional morality of so much religion which seems designed to preserve the status quo.

Yet many of P's first readers would have found the first chapter of Genesis rather a shock. In the ancient Near East, this vision of the creation was radically new. God appears in the very first sentence without any introduction. P uses the formal divine title "Elohim," a term that sums up everything that the divine can mean for humanity. In a world where there were many deities, a reader would be likely to ask, "Which god are we talking about?" or "What is Elohim?" Most of the Near Eastern deities had parents and complex biographies that distinguished them from one another, but P introduces his Elohim without telling us anything about his origins or past history in primordial time. The pagan world found the timeless world of the gods a source of inspiration and spirituality. Not so P, who ignores God's prior existence As far as he is concerned, his God's first significant act is to create the universe. Again, the very notion of a wholly omnipotent deity was a new departure. All gods in the Near East had to contend with other divine rivals. None had a monopoly of power. It was a belief that expressed the tragic realism of the pagan vision, which recognized life's complexity and could not admit the luxury of a final solution. Pagans could not imagine a deity who could set all things to rights. P's claim that his god can provide the *only* solution to life's ills is daring; his strict monotheism is also a new departure in Israel, since hitherto most Israelites had recognized the existence of other gods.

When pagans reflected on the creation of their tragic world, they could not imagine the gods creating the cosmos without a good deal of effort. Marduk, the god of Babylon, for example, only managed to bring the earth into being after fighting a mighty battle with the goddess Tiamat, the primal sea. He had split her carcass in two, as though she were a giant shellfish, in order to form the earth and sky out of her body. The myth expressed the pagan conviction that no ontological gulf separated the sacred sphere from the mundane. The gods, human beings, and the natural world were all composed of the same divine substance and shared the same predicament. The primordial violence of chaos and formlessness could always return, and human beings had to share in the gods' endless struggle to keep them at bay. We know that the Israelites told similar stories about their God's battles with a sea monster called Leviathan and a fearful dragon named Rahab when he had created the world.[1] But P apparently cannot countenance the idea of his all-powerful Elohim having to contend with rivals. In his poem, the sea monsters are simply God's creatures, and instead of having to slaughter them, he gives them his blessing. Indeed, P seems to be embarked on a polemic against the dominant religious ideas of his time. Since the eighth century BCE, some Israelites had worshipped a host of astral deities alongside their own god, Yahweh, but in P's poem the sun, moon, and stars are given a purely functional role, "to separate the day from the night; and let them be for signs and for seasons and for days and years" (1:14).

At the end of the creative process, God, having expended no effort, was not exhausted by his labors. He brought his work to an end, and on the seventh day he rested and contemplated his creation. Other creator gods built temples as a sign of their victory over the wild forces of chaos, but P imagines his God instituting the Sabbath rest instead. This will be a temporal shrine in which the people of Israel can rest from their labors each week with their God. The Sabbath was an image of stability, but it also marked the essential distinction between God and the cosmos he had brought into being. P did not share the holistic view of his pagan contemporaries: his Elohim is separate from the world and from humanity; he can regard them in rather the same way as a craftsman surveys the work of his hands. All this may have been strange to P's first readers. To most Jews and Christians today, of course, it is a familiar picture: God is in his heaven and all is right with the world.

An Initial Complexity

 YFT THE EDITORS OF GENESIS SEEM TO HAVE introduced their readers to P's vision of a serene and omnipotent deity only to dismantle it in later chapters. The God who dominates the first chapter of the Bible has disappeared from the human scene by the end of Genesis. Story after story reveals a much more disturbing God: as we shall see, the omnipotent God of the first chapter soon loses control of his creation; the immutable deity is seen to change his mind and even to feel threatened by humanity. The benevolent Creator becomes a fearful Destroyer. The impartial God who saw all his creatures as "good" now has favorites and teaches his protégés to behave in an equally unfair manner to their dependents. It is impossible to come away from the Book of Genesis with a coherent notion of God. By the time we have reached the end of the text, almost every one of the expectations we were encouraged to form in Chapter 1 have been knocked down. The editors seem to be warning us against any simplistic conception of the divine, which must always elude our limited comprehension. It is, perhaps, easy to imagine P's lofty deity as long as we place him in heaven. But in the Hebrew Bible, God does not remain wholly transcendent, locked into the celestial sphere. He enters human history and becomes inextricably involved with humanity. Once this God becomes mixed up with men and women, he frequently appears to be as ambiguous, contradictory, and dubious as they themselves.

P's poem is a masterpiece of lucidity, but it begins with a syntactical ambiguity that has long exercised rabbis, grammarians, and theologians. The first sentence of Genesis has often been translated: "In the beginning God created heaven and earth." This traditional version seems a clear statement of the doctrine—now held by all monotheists—that God created our world out of nothing: apart from God there originally existed no other substance. But in his recent translation of Genesis, Everett Fox points out that the sentence could also read:

> At the beginning of God's creating of the heavens and the earth,
> when the earth was wild and waste [*tohu va-vohu*],
> darkness over the face of Ocean,
> breath of God hovering over the face of the waters,
> God said: Let there be light![2]

The New Revised Standard Version has also chosen to interpret the verse in this way. This reading presents a very different view of the creative process. God did not make the world out of nothing, since the waste of chaos and the primal sea were already in existence, and God merely imposed order upon the *tohu va-vohu*, using this intractable stuff as the raw materials of the universe. The question of which reading is correct may prove impossible finally to resolve. Right from the start, therefore, Genesis implies that we will find no clear-cut doctrinal statements in its pages. Also, one of these interpretations, at least, challenges one of our most basic religious beliefs, by suggesting that God was not responsible for the creation of primal matter. The fact that the Bible begins with a sentence that can be—and has been—read in two different ways warns us that we will often have to struggle to make sense of Genesis. We are dealing with ineffable matters, and a wholly straightforward style may not always be appropriate.

In all cultures, human beings have been fascinated by the mystery of existence. Their creation myths were not designed as factual accounts of the origin of life but expressed their wonder that anything should exist at all. The Vedas suggest that not even the gods could understand how reality emerged from the abysmal nothingness of the beginning. P's ambiguous opening sentence shows that he also understood that when we contemplate the dark world of uncreated reality we are entering a realm where simple, consistent statements will not suffice. As early as the eleventh century, the great Jewish commentator Rashi pointed out that the first chapter of Genesis did not describe a literal sequence of events. If God created light on the first day, what was made on the fourth? Did he create seeds on the third day or on the sixth? P is quite unconcerned about such anomalies. He was not attempting a scientific account of the creative process but trying to show his readers how they should view their world.

Blessing

 FIRST, P WANTED TO SHOW THAT THE COSMOS was an ordered place: lawfulness had prevailed over the primal confusion, light over the primordial darkness, and a continent of dry land had emerged from the ocean. A habitable world had been created which could support life. P stressed the vitality of God's creation: the earth produces "plants yielding seed, and fruit trees . . . that bear fruit with the seed in it" (1:11). The waters "bring forth swarms of living creatures"; birds "fly above the earth across the dome of the sky" (1:20). When God surveyed this, he blessed his creatures, saying, "Be fruitful and multiply and fill the waters in the seas, and let birds multiply on the earth" (1:22). For the biblical writers, the natural world was not inert and dead. It shared God's own potency, teemed with life, and had its own integrity. When God blessed the earth, he gave the plants, animals, birds, fish, and human beings the power to reproduce themselves so that they too could become creative in their own way. The world was not to be exploited, therefore, but treated with the respect which belongs to any living being, imbued with sacred power. Men, women, and animals were not to devour one another. Their diet was to be vegetarian: they could eat only the leaves and fruit of the plants, while recognizing that they too shared the divine fecundity (1:29–30). Human beings did not own the world; they could not ransack its treasures indiscriminately. They were mere stewards, an insight that would be reinforced by the prescriptions of the Law of Moses and that has special relevance today, when human greed and carelessness have endangered the planet.

When P depicted his God blessing the creation, he introduced a theme that would become crucial in the Book of Genesis. In this early biblical text, the religious spirit is chiefly characterized by a yearning for blessing. Thus Jacob, it will be recalled, asked his mysterious assailant for a blessing and experienced this divine gift as an enabling power that helped him to transcend his fears and discover a new source of strength in the depths of his being. The desire for blessing thus represented a longing for the superabundant life that was apparent everywhere in the world that God had created. P made it clear that blessing was chiefly manifest in fertility: human beings and animals alike were to be fruitful, were to multiply and fill their allotted element. Their progeny would bring them immortality; they would live on in their descendants and this would enable them to transcend the constraints of time and space. This, as we shall see, would constitute the blessing sought in Israel as the highest human good. The divinely given fecundity would enable men and women to triumph over death and extinction; this blessing would help to keep the forces of chaos and annihilation at bay.

Today many religious people who embark on the religious quest are searching for a message or for privileged information that will ensure their survival in the hereafter. Others believe that religion's chief function is to provide the faithful with moral guidance. But in almost all cultures, people originally turned to religion because they wanted to live as intensely and efficaciously as possible. They knew that the world was a dangerous place and that their hold on life and health was fragile. The chaos that the gods had mastered at the beginning of time could return and annihilate the created order. Religion helped them to overcome the limitations that flesh is heir to, to experience life fully, and to put themselves in touch with the deeper currents of existence that alone could give meaning and value to the whole. The authors of Genesis experienced the divine blessing as the power which enabled all beings to live in the most profound and comprehensive sense. Men, women, animals, plants, and fish were filled with the sacred force that enabled them all to fulfill their natures and to live in their element.

Fact or Fiction?

 THE FIRST CHAPTER OF GENESIS, THEREFORE, was not intended to be a historical account of the beginning of life but a meditation upon the nature of being itself. P's poem is supremely a work of imagination. There were obviously no eyewitnesses to God's creative activity; nobody could know what he thought or said. Some Jews and Christians, in an attempt to explain how the biblical authors came by this information, have insisted that God himself dictated the text to Moses. Yet the editors of the Bible did not seem concerned with the literal viability of this creation account, since they placed immediately after it an earlier story which contradicts P in several significant respects. This version, which begins in Chapter 2:4, was written by an author (or school of authors) whom scholars call J because he prefers to call God Yahweh, the name by which he revealed himself to Moses. (In the New Revised Standard Version, the divine name Yahweh has been replaced by the periphrasis "the LORD," in the spirit of the Jewish custom of refusing, out of reverence, to utter God's name.) J could have been writing as early as the tenth century BCE, though some would give him a later date. He saw the creative process rather differently than P. First, the world was deserted and utterly empty. Then, says J, a spring rose from the earth and enabled vegetable, animal, and human life to flourish. J did not imagine God imperiously summoning all things into being, as P did. Instead, he showed God anthropomorphically fashioning the first man (*adam*) from the earth (*adamah*), working like a potter with clay. He then "breathed into his nostrils the breath of life; and the man became a living being" (2:7).

As in P, the sacred life force derives directly from God, but there the resemblance between the two accounts ends. J described humanity's first home in the Garden of Eden, which P never mentioned. His God was not distant and removed from the world. In P, male and female human beings were created together: both composed *adam:* humanity. In J's account, however, Eve was created after Adam and was inferior to him. Where P presented the world as an ordered place, J saw it as more perplexing. There were two trees in the garden: the tree of life and the tree of the knowledge of good and evil. God forbade Adam to eat from the tree of knowledge but gave no reason for this arbitrary prohibition. In P's poem, God pronounced the whole of creation to be good, but J introduced into the Garden of Eden the serpent, which persuaded Adam and Eve to rebel against their Creator. Where did this evil potential originate, and how could mere creatures find it possible to disobey a God who had hitherto seemed wholly irresistible?

The Bible makes no attempt to iron out these contradictions. Instead, it forces us to face up to the complexity of our existence. The authors could see that there was order in the universe, but they also knew that the world was a baffling place. They lived in a patriarchal society in which women were the social inferiors of men, but they were also aware that this was not the whole truth of the matter. The women of Genesis are certainly no mere helpmates, obediently subservient to their husbands. They are often forceful characters, as we shall see, and sometimes display more insight than their menfolk. By allowing these contrasting views of creation to coexist side by side, the Bible makes it clear from the very beginning that it will not give neat, tidy answers to questions that simply do not admit of a simple solution. Instead, the authors make us wrestle with the complexities of the text, and in the process we come to realize at a deeper level than before that there is no easy, straightforward path to enlightenment. We cannot treat the Bible as a holy encyclopedia where we can look up information about the divine, because we are likely to find contradictory data in the very next chapter.

Yet by presenting us at the outset with two obviously conflicting creation stories, the editors were demonstrating the basic religious principle that no one human account can ever comprise the whole of divine truth. J and P are equally inspired; both must be given equal weight, therefore, since they have different things to teach us. But if we try to interpret these texts literally, we are in a quandary: which one of these authors is right about the creation? Since J and P offer mutually exclusive versions of the creative process, we are obviously not intended to see either as historically accurate in our modern sense. Both are writing myth and fiction. In our rational, scientific culture, we tend to look askance at this type of narrative. A "myth" in popular parlance is something that is not true; a "fiction" is associated with deceit and pretense. But in the premodern world, myth was regarded as a form of psychology, which charted the inner world. In the same way, fiction can often express a truth which it is impossible to discern in the confusion of our daily lives. We have all read novels that give us fresh insight into the mysteries of human life and behavior. Sometimes they throw the hidden aspects of our experience into sharper relief and enable us to see our lives more clearly. We always enter the action *in medias res* and seldom see the *whole* shape and pattern of events: impressions and experiences jostle for our attention, and we rarely see incidents and their consequences in clear focus. Since religion is also concerned with the quest for meaning amid the chaos of mundane existence, fiction can be more useful to the spiritual life than a purely historical narrative.

By giving us two contradictory accounts of the creation, the biblical editors were indicating that both J and P were writing fiction. They offered timeless truths that could not be rendered obsolete by new cosmological discoveries. If P wanted to show us how to regard the universe in relation to the divine, J was more interested in humanity. He turned the spotlight from God in his heaven to *adam* in the garden. Above all he was concerned with the distance that seemed to separate God from humanity. How could human beings, who were sustained by the divine breath, feel that God was so remote?

Separation

 EVER SINCE ST. AUGUSTINE DEVELOPED HIS doctrine of original sin in the early fifth century CE, Christians in the West have seen the story of Adam and Eve as a catastrophic fall from perfect innocence to chronic guilt. They have traditionally equated the serpent with Satan, the fallen angel who became a devil and lured humanity away from God. Jesus died on the Cross, Christians believe, to save us from the sin of Adam, which was inherited by all human beings. But the story as we actually find it in Genesis takes a rather different view of the events in Eden. It is less concerned with morality and more interested in the existential fact of our separation from the divine source of all existence. Nearly all cultures have evolved a myth of a golden age at the dawn of time when men and women lived in close intimacy with the gods. Human beings, it was said, were in complete harmony with their environment, with one another, and with the divine. There was no sickness, no death, no discord. The myth represents a near-universal conviction that life was not meant to be so painful and fragmented. Much of the religious quest has been an attempt to recover this lost wholeness and integration. Today in our secular society, psychoanalysts frequently speak of the pain of separation, which lies at the heart of so much human distress. They regard it as a nostalgia for our prenatal existence in the womb or for our mother's breast. J's account of the Garden of Eden clearly resembles this yearning for paradise and a lost harmony. He tries to explain how the original unity with God was lost and how men and women became separated from Eden, their true home. Yet J does not regard the disobedience of Adam and Eve as unique and decisive. The separation from God was a long process, which had begun before Eve plucked the fruit from the tree of knowledge and would continue, after Adam and Eve, with each successive generation.

At first the conditions of Eden, as described by J, reflected the unity and harmony that characterize an experience of the divine. The garden was a place where God walked with human beings in the cool breeze of the evening. It was a place of blessing, a source of fertility for the whole world. Adam and Eve did not know that they were naked; they seemed unaware of sexual difference and of the distinction between good and evil. Divine and human, male and female, coexisted in such close communion that there was no consciousness of distinctions and divisions. Yet J believed that Adam had already started to become separate from God: a gap had begun to open between the divine and the human world. We have seen that the theme of separation was crucial to P's creation narrative. God created a habitable world by dividing light from darkness, sea from dry land; he blessed the Sabbath by separating it from the rest of the week and making it holy. At the end of the creation, God contemplated a world that was essentially separate from himself. In the first chapter of Genesis, therefore, separation was seen as positive and redemptive. It was a source of blessing and life. But once we have entered J's story, we find that separation could also entail irretrievable loss.

The ancient myths asserted that at the beginning of time, human beings lived in close intimacy with the gods. They talked with their deities, who gave them advice and rescued them when they were in trouble. But this clearly changed. The gods became remote from the affairs of humanity; they seemed careless of their plight. Other writers in the Near East, such as the Babylonian author of the *Epic of Gilgamesh* (c. 1250 BCE), were also concerned with this problem. When had the gods started to retreat from our world, and why had they done so? J made this the theme of his account of the early history of humanity, which we find in Genesis 2–11. He believed that once the creative process got under way, separation from God was inevitable. At a very early stage—before the appearance of the serpent and even before the creation of Eve—God had already begun to lose touch with *adam*. He could see that Adam was lonely: it was not right that he should live alone, and in an attempt to rectify the situation, J says, God created the animals. Like Adam, they were created from the earth (*adamah*), so God assumed that they would have much in common with Adam. But he had forgotten that Adam was also created in God's image and had been the recipient of the divine breath. There was a gulf between Adam and the animals that their common origin in the earth could not bridge. When God had finished creating the animal kingdom, he paraded them all before Adam. One of Adam's tasks was to give the animals names. Like God, the man had to create a meaningful world for himself by means of language; like God, he had the power to assess the natural world from the outside. But God's purpose was also to find a mate for Adam from among "all cattle," "the birds of the air," and "every animal of the field" (2:20). It is a comic picture. Like an eager match-maker, God presented the inexperienced Adam with one animal after another. Bison? Elephant? Kangaroo? We are not surprised to hear that at the end of the day, "for the man there was not found a helper as his partner" (2:20).

How could God have imagined for one moment that Adam would find a mate in this way? The God who appeared to be so omnipotent and omniscient in Chapter 1 was now unable to fathom the desires and needs of his creature. God and man were already becoming separate and incomprehensible to each other. When God finally got around to creating Eve from Adam's rib, Adam seemed to express a certain irritation. Why had it taken God so long to work it out?

> "This *at last* is bone of my bones
> and flesh of my flesh;
> this one shall be called Woman,
> for out of Man this one was taken."
> (2:23)

Eve was thus at a further remove from the divine source. God's creation was beginning to drift away from him. The cause of this separation was not sin but had been inherent in the creative process from the very beginning. As the division between humanity and God increased, sin would become a possibility, and sin, in turn, could only accelerate the dynamic of separation and estrangement.

Knowledge

 PAGANS BELIEVED THAT IT WAS DEATH WHICH made human beings different from the gods. Only the gods enjoyed eternal life. For men and women, death was unavoidable, and they had to accept their mortality. In the Bible, however, knowledge, not death, was the distinguishing hallmark of the divine. In J's story, it was the tree of knowledge, not the tree of life, that was at the center of the drama of Eden. Adam and Eve were expelled from the divine presence not because they sought an immortality denied to humanity from the tree of life but because they aspired to divine wisdom. God had seen knowledge as inseparably linked with death. When he had prohibited the fruit of the tree of knowledge, he had told Adam: ". . . in the day that you eat of it you shall die" (2:17). Yet there is a conflict here. It is true that consciousness of mortality would help to alienate humanity from the divine, but it is also true that Adam, caught as he was between the earth and his God, was bound to yearn for divine knowledge. Created in God's image, Adam naturally longed to see as a god sees. Unlike the animals, with which he could not mate, he was doomed to yearn for what was forbidden and harmful. Any image harkens after its archetype and seeks to resemble it more closely. The God who had not foreseen that Adam would long for a mate of his own species did not seem to have realized that the man also shared his own freedom of choice.

God's prohibition of knowledge is difficult for Western people to understand. Our culture has been deeply influenced by the classical literature of Greece, which saw knowledge and reason as supreme values. It is from Greece that we have inherited our prodigious thirst to find out as much as possible about the world we live in. God's command to Adam can seem perverse and obscurantist, especially since we have inherited such a catastrophic view of Adam's "fall" from grace. But the knowledge sought by Adam and Eve was not information. They were not seeking new facts, new truths, a new science. We have seen that in Genesis, human beings desired blessing before all else. They were not yet interested in unveiling arcane mysteries or wresting divine secrets from the gods.

Men and women want to live creatively, intensively, and successfully in the world. They long to fulfill the potential of their nature and rid themselves of the impediments that so often hamper their progress. But in order to live a blessed and effective life, human beings need wisdom and insight. In the Bible, wisdom and knowledge are not pursued speculatively for their own sake but are desired for pragmatic reasons. The so-called Wisdom books explore the ways in which human beings can prosper in the world. The wisdom of God makes him able to fulfill whatever he has in mind. As Job puts it:

> With God are wisdom and strength;
>   he has counsel and understanding.
> If he tears down, no one can rebuild;
>   if he shuts someone in, no one can open up.
> If he withholds the waters, they dry up;
>   if he sends them out, they overwhelm the land.
>   (Job 12:13–14)

In order to accomplish their life's purpose, men and women must be like their God. They are compelled to seek out and find the wisdom that will make them strong, happy, and effective in the puzzling world in which they find themselves. Like God, they can use this wisdom and the power that comes with it for apparently evil ends as well as for good: to destroy and imprison as well as to rebuild. What Adam and Eve sought from the tree of knowledge was not the philosophical or scientific knowledge desired by the Greeks but the practical wisdom that would give them blessing and fulfilment. Since they were programmed to be like God, it is not surprising that they were open to the serpent's suggestion that they defy their Maker and pluck the forbidden fruit.

The Possibility of Evil

 J MAKES THE SERPENT APPEAR IN THE GARDEN without any explanation. He simply tells us that the serpent "was more crafty [*arum*] than any other wild animal that the Lord God had made" (3:1). The snake is, therefore, part of God's creation, even though in Chapter 1 we saw that all created things were declared "good" by the omnipotent, all-controlling deity. But in J's story, the serpent, like man himself, was outside God's frame of reference. He was able to question God's decrees objectively. Was the serpent a part of the original *tohu va-vohu* that survived the creative ordering? If so, did the potential for rebellion and lawlessness against God lie at the root of all being? J was not a philosopher. He did not attempt to explain how evil could exist in a world pronounced "good" by a morally perfect deity. This was just one more of the imponderable problems that exist in the gracious but perplexing world that humanity had inherited. But J gives us a clear indication that there was a definite affinity between human beings and the mysterious snake. Immediately before it appeared in the garden, we are told, the man and his wife were both of them "naked [*arumim*], and were not ashamed" (2:25). The Hebrew words for "naked" and "crafty" (the epithet applied to the serpent) come from different etymological stems, but their apparent similarity here points to a connection. There is also a suggestion that it was precisely the openness and innocence of Adam and Eve that made them vulnerable to the serpent's guile.

Immediately the snake engaged in conversation with Eve, the woman, it was clear that there really was an affinity between the serpent and humanity. The two were able to relate well to each other. Indeed, the snake could also be seen as an aspect of humanity: the potential for rebellion was already present in the free will bestowed upon Adam and Eve by their Creator. In the course of the conversation, Eve showed that, like God himself, she could be inventive. The snake asked her why they had been forbidden to eat from any of the trees in the garden. Eve replied, correctly, that they could eat of all other trees, "but God said, 'You shall not eat of the fruit of the tree that is in the middle of the garden, nor shall you touch it, or you shall die'" (3:3). God had not forbidden the man and woman to touch the tree. Eve's modification of the command might seem trivial, but it was significant. It would certainly have been noted by J's first readers: in ancient literature, which often relied upon oral tradition, long speeches are regularly repeated verbatim. Already Eve, like the serpent and her spouse, had begun to drift away from God and to acquire an independent vision. The serpent tried to reassure her: "You will not die," he insisted, "for God knows that when you eat of it your eyes will be opened, and you will be like God, knowing good and evil" (3:4–5). In some respects, the serpent proved to be more truthful than God. Events would show that Adam and Eve did not die on the day that they ate the fruit: Adam lived on for nearly a thousand years. Their eyes were indeed opened, though the fruit of the tree of knowledge did not give them the divine wisdom they wanted. Instead they simply realized that they were naked, aware for the first time of their sexual difference and conscious of their desire for each other. The primal unity that had existed in the garden had been ruptured. Instead of feeling totally at one with each other and their surroundings, Adam and Eve experienced their separate identities. But they also felt their painful vulnerability. In the Bible, the word *arum* (naked) is usually used to describe somebody stripped of protective clothing and naked in the sense of being without defenses.[3] The man and woman had acquired a new knowledge of their frailty in what was becoming an increasingly difficult world.

Sin and Curse

 IN REACHING OUT TO TAKE THE FORBIDDEN fruit, Eve had become an emblem of the human desire to embrace the world and ingest experience without restraint. She saw "that the tree was good for food, and that it was a delight to the eyes, and that the tree was to be desired to make one wise" (3:6). The knowledge she sought was thus sensual as well as intellectual. Eve was striving to achieve blessing, to gain a fuller experience of life in its entirety. Later Christian commentators would blame Eve—and, by implication, the female sex—for the fall of man. Christians also became fixated on the snake, whom they identified as Satan. Yet the Bible does not dwell as obsessively on this "original sin"; after the serpent has played his part in the story, he never appears again, and, for the most part, the Jewish tradition has laid no particular blame on either Adam or Eve for the human plight. J himself was more concerned to depict the timeless human predicament: *adam* is simply "everyman"; Eve and the serpent are both aspects of humanity. We have all experienced the inner conflict that works against our best interests. Like Eve, we are greedy for life and "blessing." Like the serpent, we have an inherent tendency to question and rebel. These attributes can be destructive, but they have also been responsible for some of the most admirable achievements of men and women. J does not mean the reader to repine when he reads this story. Sin is simply a fact of life, not an unmanageable catastrophe. By plucking the fruit, human beings became conscious of their capacity for good as well as for evil.

Because these human capacities were God-given, the so-called "fall" may have been inevitable. However that may be, J was clear that sin consisted of disobedience to Yahweh. J was more concerned to show the effects of sin than to analyze its cause. Immediately, he shows, the harmony of Eden was shattered. The old intimacy with the divine was broken, for Adam and Eve hid from God when he appeared that evening in the garden. Neither would take responsibility for their sin but projected their guilt onto others. Adam blamed Eve; Eve blamed the serpent. Sin is thus shown to dissolve community; it is presented as the opposite of wholeness and integrity. Sin fragments the soul, so that human beings are no longer comfortable in their own bodies but try to hide their nakedness. This fragmentation can only spread dissolution and infect the whole environment. Today we are not always comfortable with a virtue that consists entirely of obedience. It seems a denial of human autonomy and an unworthy subservience to an external authority. But perhaps we can see the sin of Adam and Eve as a refusal to accept the nature of things. Eve had sought blessing, but, Genesis teaches us, this is not something that we can grab for ourselves without heed for the consequences. J would reinforce this insight in the story of the Tower of Babel. A lust for life can be an expression of rampant egotism and a desire for self-aggrandizement which takes no care for the rest of the world.

In Genesis, as we shall see, obedience leads to blessing. Sin, on the other hand, leads to curse. If the blessed human being is at ease in the world and knows how to live there effectively and harmoniously, the cursed man or woman experiences only failure. They will know sterility, paralysis, and defeat on the spiritual as well as on the physical plane. After their sin, God cursed Adam and Eve. When he had blessed them, he had promised them fertility. Now, he told Eve, "I will greatly increase your pangs in childbearing." The primal harmony and love between the sexes was over for ever: "your desire shall be for your husband," God told Eve, "and he shall rule over you" (3:16). As for Adam, he would no longer be a source of blessing for the world.

> ". . . cursed is the ground because of you;
>   in toil you shall eat of it all the days of your life;
> thorns and thistles it shall bring forth for you;
>   and you shall eat the plants of the field."
>
> (3:17–18)

Eden had been a source of blessing and fertility for the earth. Now the earth itself had become sterile. The thorns and thistles of the desert would invade the human enclave. In the Bible, the desert is habitually associated with the primal chaos which God had dominated when he brought the cosmos into being. In the Hebrew imagination, the desert was an empty waste, like the original *tohu va-vohu,* a realm of nonbeing which constantly threatened to annihilate humanity's fragile achievements.[4] Because they refused to accept the limitations of their existence, Adam and Eve had become a curse to one another and to their surroundings. The loss of blessing meant that they were no longer able to live productively and harmoniously in the world.

The curse of Adam and Eve has a sad relevance for us today. We have seen that human fertility was the chief characteristic of a blessed person. In an age when infant mortality was high and childbearing perilous, abundance of progeny was understandably prized. It was, in many cultures, experienced as an effective counterweight to the threat of mortality and extinction. But in our own day, when our greed for a fuller and more productive life has led to a selfish rape of the planet, childbearing and fertility have become a potential danger as we face a population explosion of fearful proportions. Like Adam, we are threatened with a new desert, a new sterility, a world in which human beings cannot easily live. Like Eve, we have reached out eagerly for blessing, refusing to accept the limitations of the environment and in the nature of things. Hence we have become a curse to our world. Our curiosity, refusal to accept the status quo, and ceaseless questioning have not been wholly bad, since they have enabled more people than ever before to live better and more effective lives. But our scientific and technological achievements have also brought devastation. Our knowledge has been for evil as well as for good.

Genesis is a story of beginnings. We can see that in Adam and Eve, humanity was starting to grow up. Human beings cannot live in the womb forever; they have to be ejected from Eden and become separate individuals, forced to make their own way in an alien world. After their sin, we watch Adam and Eve behaving like children or young adolescents, unable to cope with their new powers and responsibilities. From being naked and innocent, like newborn infants, men and women have to become crafty, like the serpent, in order to survive. There can be no going back to Eden. God "drove out the man; and at the east of the garden of Eden he placed the cherubim, and a sword flaming and turning to guard the way to the tree of life" (3:24). There is no hope of immortality. But the Bible does not see this as impossibly tragic. The story of Adam and Eve is simply a starting point that does not overshadow the rest of the narrative, as it has tended to do in the Christian imagination. The golden age of Eden is seen as a phase of life that human beings have long since left behind, for good as well as for ill. Throughout Genesis, the editors have included long genealogies of Adam's descendants. These trace the rise and fall of one generation after another as well as the passing of the centuries that take human history forward and separate it inexorably from paradise. Intercourse with God will no longer be easy for men and women; instead they will have to struggle to make sense of God's world for themselves and catch only glimpses of an increasingly distant and puzzling deity. Genesis will show the gulf between the divine and the mundane increasing, and God withdrawing ever more completely from the human scene. Yet all was not lost. Before Adam and Eve left the garden, God made clothes for them out of animal skins. They did not begin their journey into our world without enjoying some measure of divine protection.

Cain and Abel

 IN THE SPACE OF TWO SHORT CHAPTERS, GOD has changed. The omnipotent deity was no longer in control of his creation; eager to bless his creatures, he was forced to curse them. Having pronounced the world to be good, God had discovered that some of the qualities he had given to humankind lead to evil and destruction. In the story of Cain and Abel, Adam's two oldest sons, God appears in an even more dubious light. Cain, the farmer, and Abel, the herdsman, both offered sacrifice and homage to God, but God, without giving any reasons for his preference, found only Abel's offering acceptable. Immediately, we are told, Cain became "very angry, and his countenance fell" (4:5); the Hebrew implies that his face crumpled and fell like that of a child in shock and sorrow. But God was entirely unsympathetic, uttering an obscure and cold sentence. "Why are you angry, and why has your countenance fallen?" he asked Cain. "If you do well, will you not be accepted? And if you do not do well, sin is lurking at the door; its desire is for you, but you must master it" (4:6–7). Again, we have to wrestle with the meaning of the text. In some translations, God tells Cain to hold his head high: like an impatient parent or teacher, he briskly urges Cain to grin and bear his disappointment. The next step is up to him. Evil was a fact of life, a crouching demon, lying in wait for humanity, but, the Hebrew further suggests, human beings also yearn toward evil, as Eve hungered for the forbidden fruit. God gave no reason for his rejection of Cain and his gift; he simply told him that he had the power to resist the surge of anger and rage rising in his heart.

God spoke as though evil were an objective power, independent of both himself and of Cain. Yet we cannot help feeling that God himself bears some responsibility for what happened. This is not the impartial God of classical theism; this is not the God of whom Jesus would say, "he makes his sun to rise on the evil and on the good, and sends rain on the righteous and the unrighteous" (Matthew 5:45). Teachers, rabbis, and pastors constantly insist that God loves us all equally, whatever our failings. But this is not the God who has spoken to Cain. This God is grossly unfair and has favorites. One of the main themes of Genesis, as we shall see, is God's partiality. Habitually the younger son is preferred by both God and his parents, a choice which reverses the natural order of inheritance and underlines the arbitrary nature of the divine favor.

Most readers can empathize with Cain's rage and dismay. One of the most painful lessons that we have to learn in life is that the apportioning of love is neither fair nor rational. Some people have the gift of inspiring affection and others do not. Those who are unloved may have excellent qualities and be more admirable than those who are preferred. As a result of their rejection, they can become even more unlovable. This hard fact of life, which can affect our whole orientation, is usually first revealed to us while we are growing up in the family circle. It is therefore fitting that one of the main features of the Genesis story, which traces humanity's coming of age, is sibling rivalry, which often expresses itself in murderous rage. Unless human beings can bring themselves to accept this early familial injustice and make their peace with it, they will remain fixed in vengeful patterns learned in childhood and will never progress to maturity and freedom.

In this story, God behaves like the most inept of parents. The tale probably originated as an attempt to explain the enmity that often exists between pastoralists and agriculturalists, but J has given it a darker, more archetypal significance. God's ways are becoming increasingly obscure to human beings. In his commentary on the story, one of the rabbis makes Cain say: "There is neither justice nor Judge [in this world]."[5] If God himself is unfair, the world can make no ultimate sense. We have all felt the bewilderment of Cain when faced with the arbitrary injustice of life. The heavens seem closed, and God—if God there be—appears to have turned his face away for no good reason. Cain himself could not master his grief and fury. Instead, "Cain said to his brother Abel, 'Let us go out to the field.' And when they were in the field, Cain rose up against his brother Abel, and killed him" (4:8). Cain and Abel were adults, but Cain carried through what many older children long to do when they have been replaced by the birth of a younger brother or sister.

The biblical author makes no attempt to exonerate God or to explain his behavior. Indeed, he seems to be going out of his way to imply that no such explanation is possible. All we can do is to confront the apparent injustice of God with fortitude, to hold up our heads and resist the temptation to add to the world's ills. It is a bleak message and a reminder that biblical religion does not offer an unrealistic panacea to readers. Once Abel was dead, God proved rather belatedly that there *was* some justice in the heavens. Cain, whom he had pushed to the limits, was cursed; he could no longer till the ground but must become a nomad, wandering ceaselessly in search of sustenance. In despair, Cain cried aloud to this implacable God:

"My punishment is greater than I can bear! Today you have driven me away from the soil, and I shall be hidden from your face; I shall be a fugitive and a wanderer on the earth, and anyone who meets me may kill me." (4:13–15)

Sin, which is shown here to be murderously destructive of community, leads to a widening of the gulf between God and humanity. The cursed man becomes an exile from the rest of the human race. Human beings are beginning to be seen as displaced people, alienated from the world, unable to live productively or harmoniously in it and marching ever farther from an increasingly distant and dubious God. Adam had been exiled from Eden; now his oldest son was forced even farther from the divine, into the land of Nod (wandering). Yet like Adam, Cain did not go into exile without some measure of divine protection. God did not approve of capital punishment for this murder: Cain was marked with a sign, "so that no one who came upon him would kill him" (4:15).

The "Evil Inclination"

 IN THEIR EXILE, CAIN'S FAMILY IS SAID TO HAVE created civilization. Cain "built a city, and named it Enoch after his son Enoch" (4:17). His great-great-great-grandsons were also originators of cultural attainments: Jubal was "the ancestor of all those who play the lyre and pipe," and Tubal-cain "made all kinds of bronze and iron tools" (4:21–22). Genesis, however, seems to take a very negative view of civilization. The book's authors see it as the work of the first murderer, and a mark of humanity's exile from the divine. Other Near Eastern traditions were, by contrast, highly critical of the gods, while they regarded human culture as an absolute value. Where clothing is a symbol of loss in the story of the Garden of Eden, in the *Epic of Gilgamesh* it is a sign of progress and development. Gilgamesh is consoled for the loss of immortality by the splendid architecture of Uruk, the city of which he is king; he is urged to take pride in its architecture and achievements. And the biblical view conflicts as well with our own Greek heritage, which glorified the achievements of the *polis.*

Yet we should beware of branding cities and civilizations as "evil" or "sinful" in the Christian sense. As we have seen, the Jewish tradition has a more pragmatic attitude toward sin, regarding it as an unfortunate fact of life. In the Talmud, the Rabbis refer to the "evil inclination" (*Yeytzer ha'ra*). This did not mean a chronic yearning for absolute wickedness. It was closer to what Freud would later describe as libido, an instinct for life that is the source of our energy and desire. The "evil inclination," as we have seen, could be creative. The Rabbis noted that on the sixth day of creation, God pronounced his work to be *"very good"* and concluded that this was the day on which he had created the evil inclination in humanity:

> *And behold it was very good.* This is the evil impulse. Is the evil impulse good? Yet were it not for the evil impulse no man would build a home, nor marry a wife, nor beget children, nor engage in trade. Solomon said: "All labor and all excelling in work is a man's rivalry with his neighbor."[6]

By attributing the civilized arts to the descendants of Cain, the restless wanderer, the Bible recognized that civilization is built as well as destroyed by anger and discontent. Much of our God-given energy can erupt in creativity and the life-enhancing arts as well as in uncontrolled hatred and egotism. The secret is to learn how to master and channel the power that lies coiled at the root of our nature, waiting to spring and recoil upon us. Instead of using it like Cain to destroy, we can deflect it and make it a source of blessing.

The Flood

 IN SEVERAL NEAR EASTERN EPICS, THE CRE-
ation of the world was followed by a great flood which
destroyed the entire population, with the exception of a
few divinely favored individuals. In the *Epic of Gilgamesh,* the Flood
was seen as a turning point in history; it was the moment when the
gods and humanity decided to go their separate ways. Before the
Flood, the gods had been enraged by the noise made by human
beings, which disturbed their slumbers. For this entirely frivolous
reason they decided to destroy the world, though one of the gods
arranged for his favorite man, Utnapishtim, to be spared. Yet when
they saw the horrifying devastation of the Flood which they had
unleashed upon the world, the gods were ashamed. Henceforth, by
common consent, gods and mortals parted company. It was clearly
dangerous and undesirable for divine beings to meddle in mundane
affairs. The gods would have no more direct contact with human
beings; instead, men and women would concentrate on building
their own civilizations here on earth.

The biblical writers, however, believed that the radical break with
heaven occurred when Adam and Eve were banished from Eden, so
J and P (whose versions have been merged by the editors) had a
rather different perception of the Flood. They both blame human
beings for the deluge. It was not God's fault. He "saw that the
wickedness of humankind was great in the earth, and that every

inclination of the thoughts of their hearts was only evil continually"
(6:5). It was a complete reversal of the creation story, when God had
declared that the whole world was good. Now, P tells us, when God
looked upon the earth, it "was corrupt; for all flesh had corrupted its
ways upon the earth" (6:12). He therefore resolved to destroy the
world, sparing only Noah, who was "a righteous man, blameless in
his generation" (6:9). Accordingly, the springs of the primal Ocean
were opened and watery chaos was allowed to resume control:

> Everything on dry land in whose nostrils was the breath of life died.
> He blotted out every living thing that was on the face of the ground,
> human beings and animals and creeping things and birds of the air;
> they were blotted out from the earth. Only Noah was left, and those
> that were with him in the ark. (7:22–23)

It is a shocking moment; nothing has prepared us for this merciless
divine violence. We have seen that human beings are sinful, but we
have also seen the pathos of the human condition. Indeed, it has
appeared that the conflict in the human heart is at least in part
attributable to the Creator. Now as we watch the Creator God
becoming a Destroyer, it is hard to feel that the deity of the Flood is
anything but evil.

The biblical authors insist that God is not to blame. J tries to
emphasize Yahweh's pain: he "was sorry that he had made
humankind on the earth, and it grieved him to his heart" (6:6). It is
another blow to the serene image of the God depicted in Chapter 1,
who could never have changed his mind in this way. At best, the God
of the Flood can be seen to behave like a petulant child who is tired
of the castle he has created with his building blocks and knocks it
down. At worst, he appears like those tyrants and dictators in our
own century who have assumed godlike powers and have attempted
to purge the world of what they regard as evil. Yet by the end of the

story, this seemingly immature and cruel God has changed. We will see that he has to learn to accept the "evil inclination" that he created in the hearts of human beings.

Noah

 BUT WHAT ARE WE TO MAKE OF NOAH? HERE again, the biblical writers present us with an enigma. On the one hand, Noah is introduced as a pivotal figure. He was the first man to be born after the death of Adam; and he comes exactly midway in the genealogies between Adam and Abraham. From the start, he was seen as a source of consolation for accursed humanity. At his birth, his father, Lamech, cried: "Out of the ground that the Lord has cursed this one shall bring us relief from our work and from the toil of our hands" (5:29). There were hopes that he would reverse the curse of Adam's sin and bring relief to both humanity and the afflicted earth. Yet it is difficult to see what is so special about Noah. P, who tells us that Noah was a *tzaddik,* a righteous man, qualifies this by suggesting that he was merely outstanding among his notoriously evil contemporaries. It seems rather faint praise. When J introduces Noah, he simply tells us that "Noah found favor in the sight of the Lord" (6:8), but does not mention his virtue. Is this yet another case of God's arbitrary favoritism? If so, God's actions seem even more terrible, since there appears to be no valid ground for the choice of Noah out of the whole of humanity. Why save this man and his family and exterminate everybody else?

However we choose to view Noah's "righteousness," it does not seem to include concern and compassion for his fellow human beings. Unlike Abraham in similar circumstances, Noah did not plead for his contemporaries when he was told of God's plan to destroy the world. When God informed Abraham that he was about to destroy the cities of Sodom and Gomorrah because of the evil behavior of their inhabitants, Abraham would beg God to spare them, insisting that if as few as ten good men could be found in Sodom, it was God's duty to spare the city. It was a question of justice. "Will you indeed sweep away the righteous with the wicked?" Abraham would ask in horror. ". . . Far be it from you to do such a thing, to slay the righteous with the wicked, so that the righteous fare as the wicked! Far be that from you! Shall not the Judge of all the earth do what is just?" (18:23, 25). This was similar to the question that the rabbi put onto the lips of Cain. When we look around at the suffering world, we are often outraged by the pain inflicted on apparently innocent people. They are starved to death in terrible famines, massacred by tyrants and bullies, impoverished by mercenary governments. Abraham's courageous plea for the innocent should empower us to cry aloud to heaven in protest and not accept facile or glib theologies that seek to smooth our horror away. Abraham voiced our own concerns in this incident. He emerged from this intercession as a man of compassion, capable of deep moral courage. He would risk the wrath of God rather than stand idly by while a great injustice was perpetrated. He was already possessed of the fearless passion for righteousness that would inspire the great prophets of Israel. We long for such a voice at the time of the Flood. Surely a truly righteous man would stand up and plead for hapless humanity, not to mention the entirely guiltless birds and animals. Yet unlike Abraham, Noah did not speak up. He simply carried out instructions, saved himself, his immediate family, and the requisite members of the animal kingdom. As far as we can tell from the text, he did not even consider smuggling a few of the doomed men and women onto the Ark.

What kind of righteousness is this? Noah simply did what he was told, asked no questions, and saved his own skin. Blameless only "in his generation," Noah shows that as yet humanity's ethical ideal was undeveloped. Even God did not seem to understand the nature of human goodness. Later, all the great world religions, including Judaism and Christianity, would come to the conclusion that practical compassion was the chief religious duty and the hallmark of all true spirituality. Noah's virtue, however, consisted in obeying the rules. The original title of Thomas Keneally's novel *Schindler's List* was *Schindler's Ark*. The image of the Ark was highly appropriate for Oscar Schindler's factory, a safe haven for hundreds of innocent potential victims of the Nazi Holocaust. A playboy and a philanderer, Schindler was no "righteous man" in the conventional sense of the word: he would almost certainly have been condemned to death by the vengeful God of the Flood. Yet ultimately he proved to be more righteous than Noah, risking his own neck to rescue people deemed unworthy of life by his society and peers. Most of Schindler's contemporaries behaved like Noah, blocking out all knowledge of the carnage that was being perpetrated around them, obeying orders in order to save themselves and their immediate families. The best that many could do was to ride out the storm in safety.

The Ark

THE ARK ITSELF, A SEALED BOX WITH ONLY one skylight giving access to the outside world, is an apt image of that kind of blinkered mentality. It is significant that Noah's Ark is often given to children as a toy. When we think about this story, we tend to concentrate on the haven of the Ark and forget about the horror of the Flood itself. Poussin's picture *The Deluge* is a useful corrective: we scarcely see the Ark. Instead we focus on the despair and terror of the men and women who are about to be drowned. All too often, religion encourages us to concentrate on those who are safely within the fold to the neglect of the rest of suffering humanity. Some theologies, such as Calvinism, seem to revel in the notion that only a few people are "elect" and the vast majority of the human race is condemned to eternal death. But Genesis does not condone such an attitude. "Am I my brother's keeper?" Cain asked defiantly after the first murder (4:9). The reader, confronted with the man who was the first to take such selfishness to its ultimate and logical extreme, can only answer Cain with a decisive "Yes!"

In the older Flood stories, gods and humans alike were overwhelmed when they saw the devastating effects of the deluge. In the *Epic of Gilgamesh*, Utnapishtim, the sole survivor, recalled his desolation when he finally climbed out of *his* Ark:

> . . . stillness had set in,
> And all of mankind returned to clay.

> The landscape was as level as a flat roof.
> I opened a hatch, and light fell on my face.
> Bowing low, I sat and wept,
> Tears running down my face.[7]

Like many of the survivors of the Holocaust, Utnapishtim felt no elation at having been spared. We know that, on the contrary, survivors often feel acute guilt or even despair. When life as they know it has been destroyed, they can find neither sense nor meaning in their continued existence. Noah, however, expressed no such horror when he stepped out of the Ark and surveyed the devastated landscape and the bloated bodies of the Flood's victims. He seemed to experience no distress when he gazed upon the empty world, to feel no ambivalence about the divine cause of the catastrophe. He obediently led his family out of the Ark, released the animals, and, without hesitation, offered a sacrifice to his God, the Destroyer. Nor did God betray the same kind of distress as the gods of Mesopotamia; instead, he showed only perfunctory regret:

> Then Noah built an altar to the Lord, and took of every clean animal and of every clean bird, and offered burnt offerings on the altar. And when the Lord smelled the pleasing odor, the Lord said in his heart, "I will never again curse the ground because of humankind, for the inclination of the human heart is evil from youth; nor will I ever again destroy every living creature as I have done." (8:20–21)

It was fortunate that God liked the smell of roasting meat. His change of heart did not come as a result of anguished reflection; it seemed a casual response to Noah's flattering offering. It is tragic that this new divine tolerance came too late for the rest of the human race.

It is hard to feel that the reaction of either Noah or his God is adequate. God's newfound compassion seems as arbitrary as his wrath, and Noah appears to be a little too ready to offer homage to a deity who has shown such monstrous cruelty. The twentieth century has been one long holocaust. We have seen too much massacre and genocide to condone such behavior in our God. Believers who rush to God's defense here should reflect that if we excuse a deity who almost destroys the entire human race, it is all too easy to justify earthly rulers who have undertaken similar purges. Genesis does not offer a smooth, consistent image of God. It reflects the anguish of humanity as it struggles to adapt to a world that seems more and more dangerous and unpredictable. As God becomes more remote and the earth more populous and complex, human beings can see only puzzling, ambiguous glimpses of the divine.

The German historian Rudolf Otto described the sacred as a mystery that was at one and the same time terrible and fascinating; it can fill us with dread, as well as exerting an irresistible attraction.[8] The Flood is an example of the dreadful power of the divine, and we should feel repelled by this fearful story. When we contemplate the tragedy of a world convulsed repeatedly by natural catastrophes which wipe out thousands of innocent people, to say nothing of the atrocities committed by human beings, it is very hard to believe that there is a benevolent deity in charge of the world. The authors of Genesis do not attempt to deny the theological difficulties inherent in monotheism. We should not construct a theology that is so facile that it enables us to blunt our sense of life's horror and cruelty; rather we should admit that, like Jacob, we have to wrestle painfully in the dark before we can discern the divine in such circumstances.

After the Nazi Holocaust, for example, some Jews came to the conclusion that the benevolent, omnipotent, and personalized God of classical theism had died in Auschwitz. That did not mean that they had abandoned the painful quest for meaning, however. There is a story that one night in Auschwitz a group of Jews put God on trial and found him guilty for permitting the obscenity of the camps. They condemned God to death. When the trial was over, the presiding rabbi announced that it was time for the evening prayer. Ideas about God can die, but the search for faith and ultimate value in a terrible world continues, even in the presence of the worst horror. After such catastrophe, silence seems a more appropriate response than Noah's instant and apparently unthinking sacrifice to the deity who had inflicted mass destruction on an unprecedented scale.

One of the problems of monotheism has been its reluctance to accept evil in the divine. But if we cannot admit that there is evil in God, it is very difficult for us to accept the evil we encounter in our own hearts. It means that we can make evil inhuman and monstrous, as in the Christian image of Satan. Another possible response is to justify the cruelties of the world by attributing them to an omniscient God "who knows best." This, in turn, can make human violence acceptable and can even give a divine rationale for the atrocities of dictators who assume godlike powers. Hindus say that evil is one of the masks of God; Jewish Kabbalists also located the source of evil in a trauma in the divine sphere. When we confront the huge pain of the world, we are up against a dark mystery. We are in what the mystics have called a cloud of unknowing and should not expect to see a silver lining immediately.

The New Adam

ANOTHER WAY IN WHICH HUMAN BEINGS have shielded themselves from the ubiquitous mystery of evil has been to deflect it from themselves and from "God" onto others. This is the strategy adopted by Noah after the Flood. God, at least, had learned something from the disaster. He repeated the phrase "never again," the watchword of many Jews since the Nazi Holocaust. He was ready to make a new beginning. The biblical writers cast Noah as the new Adam. Like the first human beings, he and his sons were commanded, "Be fruitful and multiply, and fill the earth" (9:1). They were reminded that "in his own image God made humankind" (9:6). The reader cannot help wishing that God had reflected a little more deeply on the sanctity of human life before deciding to exterminate the race. The tragedy of the Flood had taught God that he must come to terms with the evil inclination in humanity. He entered into a covenant agreement with Noah, vowing that he would "never again" interfere with the natural order.

But our hopes for the new Adam are short-lived; almost immediately we have to watch Noah's fall from grace. Like Adam, he was a "man of the soil," and was "the first to plant a vineyard" (9:20). After drinking some of the wine, he became intoxicated and fell into a drunken stupor. His youngest son, Ham, saw Noah lying naked in his tent and went with the news to his two brothers, Shem and Japheth.

They piously "took a garment, laid it on both their shoulders, and walked backward and covered the nakedness of their father; their faces were turned away, and they did not see their father's nakedness" (9:23). Adam and Eve had experienced their naked vulnerability after the fall, but Noah's grotesque nudity lacks their pathos. It is a sign of the decline of humanity since Eden. Noah, the "righteous man," lacked the spiritual resources to survive the trauma of the Flood. Damaged by his experience, he abused himself, his children, and the gift of the vine. When he woke, he refused to take responsibility for his state but immediately projected his guilt and self-disgust onto an innocent party, his grandson Canaan, the son of Ham:

> When Noah awoke from his wine and knew what his youngest son had done to him, he said,
>
>> "Cursed be Canaan;
>> lowest of slaves shall he be to his brothers."
>
> (9:24–25)

Some of the worst atrocities of history have occurred as a result of this type of scapegoating, when we blame others for our own crimes and inadequacies. In the imagination of Western Christians, for example, Jews and Muslims were both seen as shadow-selves of Europeans at the time of the Crusades. Christians accused Jews of murdering little children and mixing their blood with the matzoh bread of Passover; it was a fantasy that reflected Christian anxieties about the Eucharist and displayed an almost Oedipal fear of the parent faith. At the same time, Christians accused Islam of being a murderously violent and intolerant religion at a time when *they* were fighting their own brutal holy wars against Muslims in the Near East. There were similar projections in Nazi Germany. Noah's curse of Canaan inspired the same type of cruelty. It provided a rationale for Israel's later subjugation of the Canaanites and the proposed genocide of the native peoples of the Promised Land, as described in the Book of Joshua. Later still, Christians would point to this verse to justify the institution of slavery: Africans were believed to be the descendants of Ham and were thus condemned to be the "lowest of slaves" to their fellow human beings. God had scourged and purged the human race, and now Noah, his favored survivor, passed the mantle of suffering on to others.

Yet again, God's plans had been foiled. Noah had not brought consolation to the human race. Instead of being a source of blessing, he had become, like the first Adam, a curse to others. His righteousness had proved inadequate. Sealed off from the disaster in the Ark, he had denied the unfolding horror around him. After the Flood, he remained in denial, shutting out the devastated world in a self-induced stupor. But despite his survival, Noah was himself a victim of the divine violence, and his story shows us that a new start based on violence and the destruction of a people cannot usher in a healthy world order. Readers of Genesis are forced to consider the unwelcome fact that they are all descended from a drunkard and an abusive father, who exposed himself to his children and neurotically disowned many of his descendants. Noah would not be the only damaged survivor, unable to assimilate his experience and wreaking his vengeance upon others.

The Tower of Babel

 WE HAVE SEEN THAT IN THE OTHER NEAR Eastern epics about the Flood, human beings and the gods decided to go their separate ways after the deluge. Yet mortal men and women were able to console themselves for this loss of divine intimacy by building their magnificent cities and founding mighty civilizations. At the end of the Akkadian *Atrahasis Epic,* the survivors of the Flood built the city of Babylon in an attempt to forge some link with the sacred. Its citizens might not be able to consort with the gods on a daily basis, as before, but they could scale the heavens by climbing their great ziggurats or temple-towers. Midway between heaven and earth, the ziggurat provided a point in this newly profane world where human beings could meet their gods. Hence they called their city *bab-ilani,* "gate of the gods."

But, as we know, the authors of Genesis had a more jaundiced view of civilization. In the story of the Tower of Babel, Babylon becomes Babel: confusion. Its builders had attempted to create, by means of a new technology, a ladder to the divine. They had baked bricks and made concrete out of raw bitumen, hoping to make new contact with the gods. "Come, let us build ourselves a city, and a tower with its top in the heavens" (11:4). Like Eve, they were attempting to seize enlightenment and godlike powers for themselves. They had forgotten that in the ancient world a holy place, which yielded access to the sacred, could not be built by human beings on their own initiative. People had to wait until the sanctity of a location was revealed to them by the gods. The builders of the tower were chiefly motivated by egotism and the desire for self-aggrandizement, and this could never be a fruitful source of spirituality. "Let us make a name for ourselves," they said, "otherwise we shall be scattered abroad upon the face of the earth" (11:4). They were attempting to build a culture that would give them an immortality of sorts, forgetting that only the gods were permitted to enjoy eternal life. By their own ingenuity, they hoped to transcend this divinely ordained boundary.

But J, the author of this story, has already made it clear that human beings cannot attain blessing by their own efforts. Civilization was a sign of humanity's separation from God. It could not renew the divine intimacy of the lost paradise. Yet again, J's God is very different from the serene deity described by P in Chapter 1. He is insecure and feels threatened by this human initiative. J tells us that when God saw humanity banding together to form a single community, he was seriously alarmed. ". . . this is only the beginning of what they will do; nothing that they propose to do will now be impossible for them" (11:6). The deity that was once incomparable and omnipotent was now disturbed by mere bricks and mortar. Yet J makes it clear that, like Eve's quest for knowledge, technology could not lead to blessing. The builders had hoped to give their mundane existence a celestial, transcendent dimension. They would thus live fuller, enhanced, and productive lives. But God destroyed this arrogant bid for divinity. He descended to earth, confused their language so that they could no longer understand one another, and scattered the people all over the earth. Once again, sin had resulted in a dissolution of community. Because of the builders' pride and egotism, the blessing turned into a curse.

The new world order planned by God after the Flood had come to nothing. If anything, humanity was now in a worse state. By making fun of the great Babylon, whose ancient civilization dwarfed his own, J showed that the worldview of his pagan contemporaries was doomed. Civilization and technology could not be a source of blessing. The next person chosen by God to give human beings a new start was born in Mesopotamia, but it would be necessary for him to leave this culture and begin afresh.

Abraham

 AGAIN, WITHOUT GIVING ANY REASON FOR HIS choice, God singled out Abram, a descendant of Noah's son Shem. His family had already migrated from the great Mesopotamian city of Ur and settled in Haran, some five hundred miles to the northwest. Then God summoned Abram:

> "Go from your country and your kindred and your father's house to the land that I will show you. I will make of you a great nation, and I will bless you, and make your name great, so that you will be a blessing. I will bless those who bless you, and the one who curses you I will curse; and in you all the families of the earth shall be blessed." (12:1–3)

Abram was to be a source of blessing for the whole world. He would reverse the curse of Adam. His blessing would be characterized by abundant progeny; displaced humanity would find a new home. At the creation, God had ordered his creatures to be fruitful and multiply; each species had been assigned to its particular element. Now

Abram must uproot himself from the old culture and give humanity a new start. His descendants would become a "great nation." He would be renamed Abraham: "Father of a Multitude." This name would become famous, not because of his great cultural achievements, but because of his numerous offspring. He would achieve the immortality desired by the builders of Babel: he would live on and his soul would expand and grow in his descendants, who would spread his benign influence all over the world. God also promised that Abraham would be supremely powerful and effective: his enemies would be cursed, doomed to sterility, frustrated and balked of success.

This blessing might seem limited and earthbound. Yet God figured prominently in the Promise. It was God who would reveal the land in which Abraham was to live, God who would enable him to succeed and to be the source of blessing. The enhanced life envisaged by Israel as the goal of the religious quest did not mean merely worldly prosperity and success. There could be no fulfillment unless a human being was open to the transcendent and the sacred. Only insofar as he lived in the presence of the divine could Abraham or his progeny be creative and effective. The sacred was not an optional extra but something that was essential to humanity. The blessing sought in Genesis would enable men and women to live wholly in accordance with their nature and fulfill their unique potential. But that would be possible only if they were in touch with the deeper, transcendent currents of existence. A blessed man or woman could be strong, vigorous, and creative only if he or she learned to live with the divine—though, as Genesis shows, it is difficult to say what exactly the divine means or what the sacred is like.

But it had never been easy for God and humanity to live together. The biblical authors make it clear that it is very difficult to live in

God's presence in this perplexing and tragic world. They would be rather surprised by the familiarity that some worshippers today claim to have achieved with God. Like many of us, Abraham lived in a violent, dangerous society. He had to wait in the dark, contending with peril, doubt, and loss. Faith was neither easy, comforting, nor life-enhancing. The divine did not reveal itself to Abraham in lucid, incontrovertible apparitions or in clearly defined doctrines. Abraham had a constant struggle to make sense of his circumstances, catching, at best, glimpses of the sacred that sometimes seemed baffling and even hostile. Blessing was neither effortlessly bestowed nor effortlessly received. Abraham's story was dominated by anxiety about the Promise, which seemed constantly in danger of miscarrying. But there was difficulty on both sides. If Abraham found it hard to live with God, God also had to learn how to accommodate himself to his new chosen people. Genesis shows that God had not found it easy to deal with the human beings he had created with such apparent facility in Chapter 1. He had lost touch with humanity at a very early stage and discovered that he could not control events. When he intervened dramatically in mundane affairs, as he did so catastrophically at the time of the Flood, God only made matters worse. He had had high hopes of both Adam and Noah. This time, he would take no chances and would submit Abraham to a long, painful probation to make sure that he was worthy of blessing.

At first God demanded unhesitating obedience from Abraham. He insisted upon a faith that entailed a ruthless abandonment of the past. Later, as we shall see, he would revise this tough policy, but never in such a way that faith became effortlessly joyful. God's initial summons to Abraham was peremptory: *Lech lekha:* Get up and go! Abraham had to leave the consolations of familiarity and tradition far behind. He had to jettison his family, his homeland, and the old ways of worship. The destination was vague. Abraham was simply to journey to "the land that I will show you," with no guarantees. How could Abraham become the father of a great nation when, as we have already been told, his wife Sarah was barren (11:30)? Abraham has been revered as a man of faith, and, in this divine summons, we see what faith requires—not only of Abraham but also of ourselves. Religious people often speak of "faith" as though it were a matter of conserving the old and traditional; they claim that it gives them absolute certainty and is not compatible with doubt. But Genesis shows that in fact faith began by demanding a radical break with the past and facing the terrors and enigmas of the unknown.

Abraham left not only his family and homeland far behind but also his gods. When he arrived in Canaan, the land of the Promise, he did not bring a Mesopotamian cult with him, nor did he attempt to impose the faith of his fathers upon his new Canaanite neighbors. Once he arrived in Canaan, he seemed to worship the local high god, El. Continually on the move, Abraham encountered El at the traditional sacred sites of Canaan: the land had to reveal its own peculiar sanctity to Abraham, and he had to respect this alien piety. He was not allowed to approach his new God with any preconceived ideas. The authors of Genesis do not show Abraham evolving a theology, a set of beliefs. Rather they imagined him responding to events and experiencing the divine in an imperative that broke down old certainties and expectations. Living with God meant, initially, that Abraham and his descendants had to be continually on the move. In the ancient world, "faith" did not mean theological conviction, as it does today, but rather a total reliance upon another. Having launched himself on this quest for the unknown, Abraham was impelled not by a set of strong, orthodox beliefs in one or another particular god but by a sense of presence that it was impossible to define or categorize. He is depicted as traveling forward toward the perpetually new, rather than taking his stand on ancestral piety.

Abraham's faith was not serene or joyful. The Promise seemed flimsy. How could he hope to live a life of blessing and fecundity in Canaan when his wife was barren, and the Promised Land full of Canaanites (12:6) and itself infertile? No sooner had Abraham and his family arrived in Canaan than they were forced by famine to leave the country and take refuge in Egypt. The Promise seemed an enigma; it referred only to the future, leaving the present insecure and unproductive. The fact that God had to reiterate the Promise so frequently only underlined this fundamental uncertainty. God seemed to be protesting too much. Abraham was often vulnerable in this new country. At one point, a band of marauders invaded the Jordan Valley and seized his nephew Lot; Abraham and his retainers had to pursue them under cover of darkness as far as Hobah, to the north of Damascus, before he was able to rescue Lot. In this frightening context, it was not surprising that the next time God appeared to Abraham, he came with a message of reassurance: "Do not be afraid, Abram, I am your shield; your reward shall be very great" (15:1).

But Abraham could find no comfort in this promise of divine protection. He asked impatiently what use were God's gifts, since he was still a childless man, with no one to inherit this reward (15:2). How could he *know* that his descendants would possess Canaan? Faith was a struggle, and God did not mind Abraham's anguished questioning. He had learned that it was hopeless to rely on such "yes-men" as Noah. Nevertheless, he merely showed the Promise in a more tragic light. Abraham fell into a trance, "and a deep and terrifying darkness descended upon him" (15:12). God then told him that his descendants would become exiles, enslaved and oppressed for four hundred years. Who needs a Promise like this? True, God also promised that he would eventually liberate his chosen people, but four hundred years is a long time, and it did not seem likely that Abraham himself would benefit.

Lot

BUT, AS WE SEE IN THE CAREER OF LOT, Abraham's nephew, appearances are deceptive. Abraham was a man of faith because, despite his moments of despair, he was a man of vision. He had the imagination to look beneath the unpromising surface of events and to realize that blessing is not always found in the most obvious places. The verb "to see" recurs constantly in the Abraham story: he was a man who had learned to look with the inner eye of the soul. Jean-Paul Sartre once defined the imagination as the ability to think of something that is not present.[9] If so, the imagination must be the chief religious faculty, since it enables us to conceive the apparently absent God. We know from our own lives that the harder, less-promising option often calls for greater creativity and gives more ultimate satisfaction. In the quest for blessing, human powers need to be engaged to the hilt if we are to achieve enhanced life.

Lot, however, was not a man of faith and therefore not blessed: he was eventually unable to function in the world and became paralyzed with fear. Shortly after their arrival in Canaan, Lot and Abraham agreed to separate: in this crowded, poorly endowed country, there was simply not enough land for two such rich pastoralists as Abraham and Lot to live together. Abraham graciously offered his nephew the first choice of territory:

> Lot looked about him, and saw that the plain of the Jordan was well watered everywhere like the garden of the Lord, like the land of Egypt, in the direction of Zoar; this was before the Lord had destroyed Sodom and Gomorrah. So Lot chose for himself all the plain of the Jordan, and Lot journeyed eastward. (13:10–11)

Abraham was left with the barren central highlands. Yet Lot, it turns out, had made the wrong choice. He pitched his tents on the outskirts of Sodom, where the people "were wicked, great sinners against the Lord" (13:13); the author reminds the reader that Sodom and Gomorrah would shortly be destroyed. In the very next chapter, marauders invade Lot's rich valley and take him prisoner. Lot was trying to find a land of blessing, like Eden, the garden of God, but he had not learned an important historical lesson. He chose to move "eastward," but ever since Adam and Eve were banished from Eden, the easterly direction had come to symbolize distance and exile from the divine presence, and without the sacred there could be no blessing.

Lot's story shows that the superficially attractive things of this world can prove to be dangerous: they can bring pain, sin, perversion, and destruction in their wake. The Promise lay with the infertile land of Canaan. Lot remained lazy and obtuse, constantly seeking the easier option. When God finally destroyed Sodom, Lot almost had to be dragged by force from the doomed city by the angels who had been sent to rescue him. They told him to "flee to the hills, or else you will be consumed" (19:17). But Lot had become too effete and citified to rough it in the open country and pleaded for a more comfortable refuge. Could he not live in the little town of Zoar? But even though Zoar was saved especially for his benefit, Lot was too afraid to settle there after he had witnessed the horrific destruction of Sodom. He and two of his daughters fled to a nearby cave and lived there in solitude, convinced that the rest of the world had come to an end. Another of Genesis's damaged survivors, Lot came to as disreputable an end as Noah. Fearing that there was no one left to marry them, his daughters made him drunk and forced him to have intercourse with them so that they could bear children.

Because he had always coasted along on the surface of reality, Lot failed to develop the inner resources to cope with the fearful things he had seen. Without the imagination of faith, he could not share the blessing of Abraham and therefore was unable to live robustly and confidently. He was no longer at home anywhere in the world. Religion has often been used to stunt a person's psychological growth or to encourage a wholly otherworldly vision. But Genesis indicates that it is the function of faith to make us more productive and more at ease with the world. God should not be experienced as a wholly etheral panacea but as a mysterious, accompanying presence that helps us to make sense of the bewildering circumstances of our life on earth.

Abraham and Pharaoh

 ABRAHAM MAY HAVE HAD VISION, BUT HE WAS no paragon. Shortly after we first meet him, we see him engaged in a shady plot to save his own life at the expense of his wife. Fleeing the famine in Canaan, Abraham took refuge in

Egypt, but he was afraid that the Egyptians would be so smitten with Sarah's beauty that they would kill him, Abraham therefore told Sarah to pretend that she was his sister. The ruse succeeded. Sarah was taken into Pharaoh's harem, and Pharaoh "dealt well with Abram; and he had sheep, oxen, male donkeys, male and female slaves, female donkeys, and camels" (12:16). In the end God had to intervene: he sent down a plague on the royal household, and when the hapless Pharaoh learned of Sarah's true identity, he returned her at once. Abraham went on his way, a rich man, "with his wife and all that he had" (12:20). Two other versions of this story were included in Genesis by the editors; they show that not all the biblical authors felt entirely happy about the patriarch's behavior here. The writer known to scholars as E (because he prefers to call God Elohim) tried to find some mitigating circumstances. He suggested that Sarah really *was* Abraham's sister, which, given the endogamous habits of this family, was not an impossibility. But J seems not at all disturbed by the patriarch's dubious ethics. Great wealth was seen as one of the marks of blessing; J stresses that Abraham's wealth consisted of livestock. The blessed man is creative: he can make his difficult circumstances work for him; living life to the hilt, he attracts life and is surrounded by living things.

Today we often see morality as central to the religious life. The authors of Genesis were certainly interested in ethics, but it was not a primary consideration for them. They do not shrink from presenting the patriarchs in an unfavorable light; they often fail to come up to the moral standards that *we* would expect to find in a man of God. J was more concerned to explore the gradual separation of God and humankind than to preach the good life. The story reminds us that the Bible does not give us clear, lucid teachings that we can apply straightforwardly to our own lives. Ethical fashions change. Today, for example, religious people are deeply concerned with what they call "family values"; they see sexual morality as crucial to the spiritual quest. But, as we shall see, the patriarchs were not family men. Whatever their other achievements, their domestic lives left much to be desired. They were frequently highly unsatisfactory as husbands and disastrous as parents. Blessing should radiate from a man who has received the divine favor to those around him, and the first people to benefit should be his immediate family. The fact that all three of the patriarchs signally failed in this is just one more indication of the difficulty of living successfully and compassionately in the divine presence.

The Friend of God

 IN EDEN, GOD HAD WALKED WITH THE FIRST human beings in the cool evening breeze, calling out to them as a familiar friend. Since then, he had made only sporadic appearances, but, J tells us, "The Lord appeared to Abraham by the oaks of Mamre, as he sat at the entrance of his tent in the heat of the day" (18:1). Looking up, Abraham saw three strange men approaching and immediately, despite the fierce sun, he ran out to greet them. In this episode, we sense the warmth, eagerness, and energetic generosity of the man. With typical Near Eastern courtesy, Abraham would not allow the men to pass until he had given them all the refreshment and comfort in his power:

> And Abraham hastened into the tent to Sarah, and said, "Make ready quickly three measures of choice flour, knead it, and make cakes."

Abraham ran to the herd, and took a calf, tender and good, and gave it to the servant, who hastened to prepare it. Then he took curds and milk and the calf that he had prepared, and set it before them; and he stood by them under the tree while they ate. (18:6–8)

All was haste, bustle, and excitement: Abraham rushed to pour out his generosity at the feet of three total strangers, falling over himself to give them his best. Yet in his world—as in our own—the stranger often represented a danger. Even today, we have to train children to be wary of strangers. Strangers were an unknown quantity. Abraham himself lived as a stranger in Canaan and recognized his marginal status there; a stranger could not rely on the protection of tribe or kin. Cain had asked, "Am I my brother's keeper?" and had been banished from the divine presence, but Abraham was ready to bring three strange men into his family home and became the first human being to enjoy an intimacy—albeit a transient one—with the divine since the expulsion from Eden.

This type of epiphany was common in the pagan world, but later Israelites, as we have seen, would deny that God could assume human form. The legend derives from a time when the religion of the Israelites differed little from that of their pagan neighbors. Yet the story was included in the Bible because it underlined a truth that would be of crucial importance in all three of the monotheistic traditions. Jews, Christians, and Muslims would all insist that practical charity to others was the most important religious virtue of all. Christians would see the apparition of Mamre as an early manifestation of God as Trinity, a revelation which had come about as a result of Abraham's eager yearning toward three fellow human beings. He bowed low before these three strangers, showing them the same reverence as to his God. As a result, God could sit and eat with Abraham as a friend.

Friendship demands a certain parity. God no longer wanted unthinking obedience from the people he had chosen. He decided to take Abraham into his confidence about his imminent destruction of Sodom and Gomorrah. Unlike Noah, however, Abraham did not scuttle obediently to do God's bidding but had the courage to argue with this frightening and notoriously unpredictable deity. The author tells us that he "remained standing before the Lord" (18:22) and begged him not to destroy the innocent with the guilty. Again, Abraham demonstrated his compassion, besides a concern for justice, pleading for the lives of total strangers in the condemned cities. Abraham had his faults, but he was capable of the disinterested love for his fellow human beings that all the great world religions have shown to be the ultimate test of true spirituality.

Family Values

 IT IS SIGNIFICANT THAT WHEN ABRAHAM pleaded for the lives of the citizens of Sodom, he made no mention of his nephew Lot, who, as we know, lived in the city. Abraham could act with exemplary charity toward total strangers, but he could be murderously cruel toward his own family, particularly his children. In this story of God's chosen family, we find very few of the "family values" that Jews, Christians, and Muslims, who all in their different ways claim to be children of Abraham, avow as crucial to the religious life. Abraham's household was a troubled one; in no way did it replicate the lost harmony of Eden.

Each generation would add to the family's suffering. Fathers, wives, sons, and brothers would revile each other, inflicting a psychic damage that frequently erupted in violence.

Abraham had been promised blessing, and that meant abundant progeny. But since Sarah was barren, there seemed little hope that God's promise would be fulfilled. This constant anxiety runs like a fault line through Abraham's story and colors his whole relationship with his God. If there were no offspring, God's promise would be null and void and Abraham's whole life pointless. This continuous anxiety demonstrates the difficulty of achieving blessing and living productively in God's presence in a flawed and tragic world. Abraham and Sarah were miserably conscious of their barrenness. "I continue childless," Abraham had cried in exasperation after Yahweh had reiterated the Promise yet again. "You have given me no offspring, and so a slave born in my house is to be my heir" (15:2–3). Sarah, now long past menopause, was frankly skeptical. When God promised that she would shortly bear a child, she simply laughed aloud. In Genesis we find no belief in the afterlife on which many religious people today base their hopes. The only immortality a man or woman could expect lay in progeny; numerous descendants alone ensured the final triumph over mortality and extinction. To have no offspring was to pour one's life into the void, the *tohu vavohu* or empty waste that God had defeated at the beginning of time. A childless life was meaningless, ending in nothingness and sterility.

This ultimate disaster was what Abraham and Sarah faced. To counter it, Sarah resorted to an expedient that was common in the Near East. She gave Hagar, her servant, to Abraham, and Hagar bore Abraham a son, Ishmael. Abraham hoped that Ishmael could be his heir. This arrangement enabled a barren woman to maintain her position as head of the household. The law code of Mesopotamia decreed that if a wife provided her husband with a woman for childbearing, he was not permitted to take a concubine of his own. But once Sarah had miraculously given birth to Isaac, she insisted that Hagar and Ishmael be sent away, even though the arrangement had been for her benefit. God also instructed Abraham to dismiss Hagar and Ishmael: he pledged that Ishmael would also be the father of a great nation, but it was Isaac alone who must inherit the blessing and the Promise. Abraham was grieved, but he obeyed. Early the next morning, he "took bread and a skin of water, and gave it to Hagar, putting it on her shoulder, along with the child, and sent her away" (21:14). With these woefully inadequate provisions, mother and child faced almost certain death in the wilderness.

In our society, a man who exposed his mistress and child to such peril would be universally condemned. There had been a ruthlessness in Abraham from the beginning. He had simply walked away from his family and his past, without a backward look. Now he was ready to sentence his firstborn son to death. The author shows the pathos and desperation of Hagar in the wilderness:

> When the water in the skin was gone, she cast the child under one of the bushes. Then she went and sat down opposite him a good way off, about the distance of a bowshot; for she said, "Do not let me look on the death of the child." And as she sat opposite him, she lifted up her voice and wept (21:15-16).

Yet again, God appears in a cruel and dubious light. As in the case of Cain and Abel, he had chosen the younger son in preference to the older, a partiality that could, once more, have been fatal to the rejected one. True, at the eleventh hour, God stepped in to rescue Hagar, providing her with a miraculous source of water. Ishmael, we read, also experienced blessing in his life: "God was with the boy" (21:20); he became a mighty archer in the desert of Paran and the father of the Arab peoples. Ishmael is one of the few survivors in Genesis who was able to come to terms with his tragic past. He did not allow the horrible truth that his father had exposed him to mortal danger to sour the rest of his life. When Abraham died, he dutifully helped Isaac to bury the father who had been ready to cut him off. Furthermore, despite his brutal ejection from the family, Ishmael continued to be regarded as a member of Abraham's household. When P described the institution of circumcision, a practice which acquired a new religious importance in the sixth century BCE, he made it clear that Abraham and his son Ishmael, who was thirteen years old at the time, were circumcised on the same day: "all the men of his house, slaves born in the house and those bought with money from a foreigner, were circumcised with him" (17:27).[10] Regarded as the cousins of Israel, Ishmael and his descendants were still regarded as honorary members of the covenant in P's time: a tragic irony in these days of hostility between Israel and the Arabs.

Abraham was also ready to do violence to Isaac, God's chosen son. God spoke to him one last time, uttering once again the phrase *Lech lekha* with which he had opened their relationship. Abraham was to get up and go to the land of Moriah to perform a terrible task. "Take your son, your only son Isaac, whom you love," God commanded, "and go to the land of Moriah, and offer him there as a burnt offering on one of the mountains that I shall show you" (22:2). We know that this was only a trial of Abraham's faith: the narrator told us at the outset that God was merely testing Abraham. But Abraham could not have known this and prepared to obey, even though the loss of Isaac would end all his hopes of blessing. The incident leaves us with difficult questions about both Abraham and his God. A deity who asks for such an extreme demonstration of devotion can seem cruel and sadistic. And why did Abraham, who had never been afraid to bargain and argue with God and who had pleaded so eloquently for the people of Sodom, not utter one word on behalf of his own son? Perhaps he was too shocked to speak: the God he had served so long had suddenly revealed himself to be a breaker of promises and a heartless slayer of children. In the face of such darkness, outrage and rebellion lose their point.

We are told nothing about Abraham's state of mind during the three-day journey to the land of Moriah. Nor are we given any clue to Isaac's reaction when it became clear that he was to be the victim of the holocaust. Did he plead with Abraham? Or did he lie down passively on the improvised altar, watching his father preparing the knife? All we know is that Abraham bound Isaac, laid him on the pyre, and "reached out his hand and took the knife to kill his son" (22:10). Perhaps he had such faith that he knew that God would intervene at the last moment, as, indeed, he did. The angel of God commanded Abraham to hold his hand. Instead of Isaac, the patriarch offered a ram, caught by its horns in a nearby bush. God renewed the Promise:

> "Because you have done this, and have not withheld your son, your only son, I will indeed bless you, and I will make your offspring as numerous as the stars of heaven and as the sand that is on the seashore. And your offspring shall possess the gate of their enemies, and by your offspring shall all the nations of the earth gain blessing for themselves, because you have obeyed my voice." (22:16–18)

Whereas Eve's disobedience had led to curse, Abraham's obedience resulted in blessing. Abraham would indeed have numerous progeny. Living on in them, he would be supremely effective; and he would enjoy the military success that was an essential part of blessing. Brought to an extremity, Abraham was promised self-transcendence.

In being ready to enter the realm of death and meaninglessness, he would enjoy life itself. He would be able to make himself at home in the world, sharing the creativity of God.

Commentators have pointed out that the story of the binding of Isaac marks an important cultic moment in early Israel, when animal oblation was substituted for human sacrifice. But the pain of the story goes beyond this liturgical relevance. It reminds us that living in God's presence requires an arduous struggle that can bring us to the brink of despair. The search for blessing, the essence of life itself, involved an encounter with death and the death of meaning. Ever since human beings had been ejected from Eden, the sacred had appeared fitfully as a powerful but ambiguous force in human affairs. The reality called "God" could manifest itself as a friendly, benevolent presence but also as terrifying and cruel. In our desperate world, where we all struggle for physical or psychological survival, our glimpses of the divine can only be fragmentary, imperfect, and colored by our experience of life's inherent tragedy. Genesis shows us a frequently shocking God, about whom it is impossible to make pious predictions.

After this supreme test, God never spoke to Abraham again, withdrawing, outwardly at least, from Abraham's life. But he was true to the Promise. Abraham enjoyed a blessed old age. Not only was he extremely wealthy but, ironically, after all his troubles with fertility in the past, he sired a whole new family. After Sarah's death, his wife Keturah bore him six sons. Right up to the end, he was productive and surrounded by life. But this time Abraham did not need God to tell him what to do. With his customary ruthlessness, he sent all his sons away, lest they jeopardize the position of Isaac, the son of the Promise. They were all dispatched far from the divine presence, to the godless realm of the east (25:6). Some of these latter-day sons were the legendary ancestors of other Near Eastern peoples. But such considerations apart, Abraham's expulsion of his sons remains disturbing. His faith benefited himself and, later, would radiate to others: to Christians and Muslims in the gentile world as well as to the Jewish people. Yet the blessing did not benefit Abraham's immediate kin, and he bequeathed to his son Isaac and his successors a tragic legacy. Many of the descendants of Abraham's discarded sons became the bitter enemies of Israel, and after Mount Moriah, Isaac and his family remained torn and conflicted.

Isaac

THE PRIMARY CASUALTY OF MOUNT MORIAH was Isaac. How do you cope with the fact that your father was prepared to kill you in cold blood? How can you relate to a deity who treats you as a mere pawn in a test of his chosen one? The Bible seems to indicate that Isaac lacked the resilience of Ishmael, his half brother. After Mount Moriah, the Bible does not let Isaac speak again until he is on his deathbed. Isaac was by far the most passive of the three patriarchs. There are virtually no stories told about Isaac in his prime: one of these is simply another version of the tale of Abraham and Pharaoh and may have been included by the editors at this point because of a dearth of Isaac material. Isaac is yet another of the survivors of Genesis who found it impossible to integrate past trauma. A mere two chapters after Abraham's death, we see Isaac as a prematurely aged, blind, and dying man—an eloquent image of a blighted existence. Isaac's life seems a blank after his father bound him on the altar and came at him with a knife. It is, perhaps, not surprising that he called God "the Fear" (31:42, 53). Freud spoke of the murderous rage that some parents feel toward their offspring. Isaac was one of those damaged children who have experienced this parental hostility to the full.

It is perhaps not fanciful to suggest that Abraham's readiness to kill his own son dealt a mortal blow to God's chosen family. What could Abraham have said to Isaac on the homeward journey? And how did Sarah react to the news that her husband had been prepared to plunge a knife into the breast of the son she had waited all her life to bear? Sarah had sometimes been skeptical about Abraham's God. Did she now recoil in horror from Abraham and his divine patron, despite the happy outcome of the test? In the very next chapter we read of Sarah's death. It is almost as though the shock killed her.

Abraham himself seemed to have little faith in Isaac, the chosen son. As he lay dying, he entrusted the steward of his household with the task of choosing a wife for Isaac. On no account must he marry a Canaanite woman; the steward must return to Haran and choose a wife from Abraham's own family. The steward asked, very reasonably: "Perhaps the woman may not be willing to follow me to this land; must I then take your son back to the land from which you came?" Abraham became quite agitated. "See to it that you do not take my son back there," he insisted (24:5–6). It is almost as though he did not trust Isaac to commit himself to the Promised Land: a mere servant had to supervise the son of the Promise. It is also significant that Abraham did not give his instructions to Isaac directly. In a book that sets great store by parental benediction, it is striking that the dying Abraham did not pass the blessing on to Isaac in person. It is almost as though Isaac did not exist for him. Or perhaps, after Mount Moriah, it was impossible for father and son to have any kind of normal relationship. We are told that Isaac grieved for his mother long after her death (24:67), but, though he dutifully buried his father when the time came, we are given no clue about his feelings for Abraham. Isaac did not die physically on Mount Moriah, but in some deeper sense his life came to an end there.

Genesis makes it clear that the religious life can involve heartbreak. It is supremely difficult to live in close proximity to the sacred and to implement a divine imperative in this puzzling and dangerous world. Not everybody who attempts it will survive. Adam, Cain, Noah, and Lot all failed and were—in different ways—damaged and alienated by this struggle. It is a sad irony that it was Isaac, another of Genesis's damaged survivors, who was chosen by God in preference to the more robust and effective Ishmael. Yet again we are faced with the unfairness of love and election. The passive Isaac is acted upon, duped, and constantly presented to us as on the brink of death. He made no discoveries as had his energetic father. We know that Yahweh blessed him and that he did inherit the Promise. Isaac "became rich" and "had possessions of flocks and herds, and a great household" (26:13–14). God himself tried to allay his fears: "Do not be afraid, for I am with you and will bless you and make your offspring numerous," he said when he transmitted the blessing to Isaac, yet it was not for Isaac's own sake but "for my servant Abraham's sake" (26:24). Even for God, Isaac remained rather a blank.

In both of the two most important scenes of Isaac's life he is lying down—on the altar of sacrifice, and on his deathbed. We find Isaac confined to that deathbed, blind and moribund, for twenty years. His life was a slow dying. In some ways, he shared the characteristics of an accursed man: he was paralyzed, passive, and deathbound. Preachers sometimes give the impression that religion will inevitably bring sweetness and light into our lives. We will feel God's love and become whole and fulfilled. Our faith will give us a consciousness of God's presence that will make us serene and joyful. But Genesis indicates that this is by no means always the case. Perhaps God had wanted Abraham to argue with him on Mount Moriah, as he had argued for the people of Sodom. Or perhaps, seeing the consequences inflicted by his "test" upon Isaac, God came to realize that too relentless a faith can lead to fanaticism and to a lack of humanity that has permanent and damaging effects upon others.

Rebekah

 GOD DID NOT RELATE EASILY TO ISAAC, WHO seemed to live in ignorance of his intentions. Instead, God chose to communicate with a woman in the generation after Abraham. Rebekah, Isaac's wife and the most powerful of the matriarchs of Israel, had all the energy that her husband so conspicuously lacked. We are struck by her purposeful activity the very first time we see her. Abraham's servant had dutifully arrived in Mesopotamia to find Isaac's bride. He had no direct divine guidance but was forced to rely on his wits. He devised a test. He told the God of his master, Abraham, that he would stand by the town well and watch the girls coming out to draw water. He would ask them for a drink, but if one of them offered to water his camels too, then, he asked God, "let her be the one whom you have appointed for your servant Isaac" (24:14).

God did not disappoint him. The first girl to appear was the beautiful Rebekah, daughter of Abraham's brother Nahor. She passed the test superbly. As soon as she had given water to the servant, "she quickly emptied her jar into the trough and ran again to the well to draw, and she drew for all his camels" (24:20). All the verbs express bustle and activity. Rebekah was constantly in motion, hurrying, hastening and rushing to the well. The text makes it clear that she had to climb *uphill* with the heavy pails of water, while the servant looked on admiringly, scarcely able to believe his luck. A Western reader may not fully appreciate the onerous nature of the test he had devised. He had brought ten of Abraham's camels with him, and camels have a huge capacity for water. Rebekah did not merely give each camel a taste but ran back and forth until they had all *finished* drinking. The last time we have seen such gratuitous and energetic generosity was when Abraham ran out to meet the three strangers at Mamre. It was Rebekah, not Isaac, who would take up the task which the dying Abraham was relinquishing, and ensure that God's blessing was passed on to the correct person.

The blessing had been imparted to Isaac, but it was still precarious and difficult to realize. It was still hard to live creatively in God's presence, as symbolized by the fact that, like Sarah, Rebekah proved to be barren. Nevertheless, God answered Isaac's prayers and opened her womb. She conceived twins. During her pregnancy, there was such turbulence in her womb that she was driven to consult God, who told her that the twins were engaged in a fateful wrestling match:

> "Two nations are in your womb,
>   and two peoples born of you shall be divided;
>   the one shall be stronger than the other,
>   the elder shall serve the younger."
>
> (25:23)

The first of the twins to be born was covered with reddish hair, so they called him Esau ("Rough One"). His twin came out grasping Esau's heel, and he was named Yaakov ("Heel-Holder"). Because of God's revelation, Rebekah knew that Yaakov, or Jacob as he is called in English, was to inherit the Promise, and when the time came she would take drastic action to make sure that he would receive his inheritance.

Jacob and Esau

 JACOB WAS BORN A FIGHTER. WE NEVER QUITE know what to make of him. He remains an enigma, his behavior sometimes shocking and disturbing, until the very last pages of Genesis. The example of Jacob makes it clear that God does not choose one person over another because of his moral virtue. Yaakov can also mean "he will deceive." His father, Isaac, accused him of acting "deceitfully" (*bemirah*; 27:35), a word which derives from the same root as the adjective *arum* ("crafty") applied to the serpent.

Yet at first Jacob seemed as passive as his father. We are told that when the brothers grew up, "Esau was a skillful hunter, a man of the field, while Jacob was a quiet man, living in tents" (25:27). Isaac loved Esau best, because he enjoyed wild game, a trivial reason which reveals a weakness for creature comforts that reminds us of Lot. Like Lot, Isaac was passive, and like Lot again, he would finally be duped by his own children. Rebekah does not seem to have told him that despite his love of Esau, God had chosen Jacob: Isaac remained in the dark. The brothers had come into the world fighting, and Isaac's blindness and neglect would cause their sibling rivalry to flare with a violence not seen since the time of Cain and Abel.

The difference between the twins became clear in the famous scene in which Jacob managed to persuade Esau to sell him his birthright (25:29–34). Esau had returned from the field, exhausted and ravenous, to find Jacob cooking a lentil stew. "Let me eat some of that red stuff," he begged his brother. Esau's language was brutish. Consumed by his agonizing hunger, he could not even recall the name for "stew." He wanted to eat some of the stuff; the Hebrew word *hil'it* is used for the feeding of animals. We might say that Esau wanted to "stuff his face" with the food. Jacob's language, on the other hand, was measured, precise, and legalistic. "First sell me your birthright," he said immediately. He wanted Esau to cede him his rights as firstborn son there and then and to seal it with an oath on the spot. "Of what use is a birthright to me?" Esau cried impatiently, and he swore the oath. Jacob handed Esau a dish of bread and lentil stew and, says the narrator, "Thus Esau despised his birthright." It was clear that Esau was not a suitable person to establish a dynasty. He was a slave of appetite, swayed by the hunger of the moment. But we are also slightly disturbed by Jacob's cold calculation. The phrase "Jacob was cooking a stew" could have a double meaning. He was indeed plotting, brewing up trouble, ready to prey on the weakness of his brother for his own advantage. How does all this guile accord with the description of Jacob as "quiet" (*tam*), a word which usually denotes innocence and simplicity in the Bible?[11] From the outset, Jacob is a puzzle to us, and we never quite feel that we know him.

The Blessing of Jacob

IN THE NEXT ACT OF THE DRAMA, JACOB SUR-
prises us yet again. When Isaac lay on his deathbed, preparing to pass the patriarchal blessing on to his favorite, Esau,
Jacob, the adroit manipulator, was no longer in control of the situation. Instead, he was ordered about briskly by his energetic mother.
Isaac may not have been informed that Jacob was God's choice, but
he should have realized that Esau had disqualified himself from
inheritance by marrying local Hittite women. It had been a condition of Isaac's own inheritance that he marry a member of his
father's family. Nevertheless, he commanded Esau to go out and
hunt some game; he intended to eat his favorite dish before giving
Esau his "special blessing." Rebekah was forced to resort to a desperate subterfuge. This time she, not Jacob, did the cooking; while
Esau was in the field, she made Isaac's favorite meal, disguised
Jacob's smooth arms with animal pelts, dressed him in Esau's
clothes, and sent him with the dish in to his father.

When clerics bless their congregation today, it can be a rather
impersonal gesture. It is possible to bless an entire congregation at
once and to give a blessing to somebody one scarcely knows. It is as
though the priest merely provides a channel for the divine power.
This is very different from the biblical notion of blessing. Isaac may
not have been as distinguished as his father, but he had been blessed
by God. Now he had to transmit this blessing to his son before he

died. Once uttered, the words of benediction could not be taken back. He was communicating his life essence to his son, breathing his very soul into the other. To do this, he had to get close to Jacob. He asked him to approach, kissed him, felt his body, and smelled his clothes. Blessing involved the body as well as the spirit. Only when this degree of intimacy had been created could he pass the power to his son. The blessing could only go to the person for whom it was intended. It is ironic and a sign of his spiritual blindness that, despite all these precautions, Isaac still mistook Jacob for the son he claimed to know and love the best. Abraham had been a man of vision; he had been able to see farther than others. Isaac lacked this insight; he had never possessed the vision that was necessary to make the blessing effective in his own life. Blessing would not work automatically; it was not magic. Later, as we shall see, Jacob himself would fail to recognize people and objects at crucial moments of his life. He too would lack the vision of Abraham, his grandfather.

Nevertheless, despite Isaac's failure of vision, the blessing *was* transmitted to the person intended by God. The words spoken by Isaac tell us more about the nature of blessing in Genesis.

> "Ah, the smell of my son
>   is like the smell of a field that the Lord has blessed.
> May God give you of the dew of heaven,
>   and of the fatness of the earth,
>   and plenty of grain and wine.
> Let peoples serve you,
>   and nations bow down to you.
> Be lord over your brothers,
>   and may your mother's sons bow down to you.
> Cursed be everyone who curses you,
>   and blessed be everyone who blesses you!"
>
> (27:27–29)

Again, the imagery of blessing evokes fertility, wealth, success, and might. The blessed individual is to live at the peak of his powers. There is also a holistic aspect of benediction: as in Chapter 1, blessing permeates the whole of the created order, linking men and nature. The blessing is designed to empower the person to bring his whole self to fruition, and at the same time it bestows the happiness and richness that will ensue from this self-realization. Blessing is intended to make a person feel at one with himself and with the rest of the world; it is a partial recovery of the lost wholeness of Eden.

The first readers of Genesis, however, may well have been perturbed by the words of Isaac's blessing. Today the same form of benediction can often be used to bless any number of different people. Not so in ancient times, when a blessing had to be appropriate for the specific person receiving it. (We shall thus see, most notably, that at the end of Genesis, when Jacob blesses his sons, each blessing is unique and adapted to the needs, personality, and destiny of the particular individual.) Since Isaac thought he was blessing Esau, the outdoorsman, the imagery of the benediction, evoking as it did the sights and smells of the fields where his elder son loved to hunt, was eminently suitable for Esau. But it was not at all appropriate for the stay-at-home Jacob, who preferred to remain in the family encampment and had no love of the open country.

Jacob was a twin, and in various cultures twins have been a common symbol of the divided self. Jacob had fought Esau in the womb. Esau was his alter ego, his polar opposite, the shadow self that, like all of us, Jacob carried within him and with whom he had to come to terms if he was to live a fruitful life. Throughout his life, Jacob found that he was unable to live comfortably either with or without his brother. His theft of the paternal blessing was in accordance with God's will, but still a dubious act. Was Jacob at all disturbed on hearing the closing words of Isaac's benediction, which cursed everybody who cursed the person who Isaac thought was Esau? Jacob had not exactly cursed his brother, but he had forever deprived him of blessing, which could be seen to come to the same thing. Would he, Jacob, now be cursed for his act of fraternal disloyalty? In some ways, we shall see that his life was indeed blighted by his failure to reconcile with Esau. Jacob was an imposter as he received the blessing, not himself. He was in disguise, clad in Esau's clothes and with his arms covered with animal pelts. It is an odd image. Jacob was trying to be both brothers at once; in psychological terms, it is almost as though he was trying to heal the conflict in his personality that would so often impede him in later life. But he received this crucial blessing with a divided, double heart. Jacob would never be able to forget the wrong he had done his brother. Until he was reconciled with Esau, his twin, and with the Esau within himself, he would find no peace. God would later ratify the blessing that Isaac had given to Jacob but, in a very real sense, the blessing spoken to Esau could never be fully effective in Jacob while he was estranged from his brother and still lacked that interior integration which is the source of all true peace and harmony.

Indeed, it soon became apparent that, despite the inspiring imagery, the immediate effect of the blessing uttered by Isaac was not peace and unity but new discord. The family that had already been polarized by the twins' rivalry was now split asunder. Where Abraham had secured the succession of Isaac by sending all his other sons away, Isaac put the whole Promise in jeopardy by failing to transmit the inheritance in an ordered manner, according to God's will. As a result, he had to send the heir away from the Promised Land. Esau was devastated by this unexpected reversal. We feel the full pathos of his position when he returns too late. "Have you only one blessing, father?" he cried in anguish. "Bless me, me also, father!" (27:38). He wept aloud, for, of course, the blessing could not be revoked. Isaac's sorrowful words outlined Esau's fate as a man without blessing: he would have to live an impoverished and conflicted life, defensive, subservient, and fruitless:

> "See, away from the fatness of the earth shall your home be,
>   and away from the dew of heaven on high.
> By your sword you shall live,
>   and you shall serve your brother."
>
> (27:39–40)

Esau was determined to kill Jacob, who was thus forced to flee to Abraham's family in Mesopotamia. The family that was supposed to reverse the curse of Babel and reunite dispersed humanity had itself been scattered and fragmented.

Jacob's Ladder

 THE PATRIARCHAL BLESSING WAS TIED INEXtricably to the land of Canaan; that was to be the element of God's chosen people, the place where they would fulfill their natures. It was to be as essential to them as the sea was to fish and the sky to birds, which God had also blessed on the day of creation and assigned a special location in the universe. It was therefore significant that on the first leg of Jacob's journey to Mesopotamia he experienced a theophany and heard God speak to him for the first time at the border of the Promised Land. In ancient religion, the cult of a holy place was associated with a nostalgia for the lost paradise, when human beings lived on intimate terms with the gods. Certain locations were experienced as numinous, as yielding access to the divine in the midst of a profane world. Jacob had reached an apparently unremarkable spot and decided to spend the night there. But in fact he had stumbled upon a "place" (*maqōm*), a word that could be translated "shrine." Unbeknownst to him, it was one of those places where the sacred had been known to manifest itself to human beings. That night Jacob dreamed of a ladder planted on the ground with its top reaching to heaven. At its summit was God, who now pronounced this solemn benediction.

> ". . . your offspring shall be like the dust of the earth, and you shall spread abroad to the west and to the east and to the north and to the south; and all the families of the earth shall be blessed in you and in your offspring. Know that I am with you and will keep you wherever you go, and will bring you back to this land." (28:14–15)

God had confirmed the blessing which Jacob had snatched from Esau. Despite the difficulties of his personal life, Jacob would enjoy the self-expansion that was ensured by numerous progeny. Above all, God would be with him on his travels, to help him to achieve success, security, and fulfillment. When Jacob woke, he consecrated the place, calling it Beth-El, the House of God. His ladder, which reminds us so forcibly of the Babylonian ziggurats, had provided him with a bridge to the divine. Jacob, who possessed the guile of the serpent, had achieved the connection with heaven that the builders of Babel had sought in vain.

God was gradually receding from the world. He would appear to Jacob far less frequently than to Abraham. For most of the time,

Jacob was like us, apparently on his own and forced to live by his wits. Jacob would have to sense God's accompanying presence by engaging with the hard reality of the world. As we know, Jacob would be renamed Israel: "One Who Fights with God." His life was to be a continuous struggle which would yield only occasional clear glimpses of the divine. In some ways, at least, Jacob would achieve the attributes of blessing. He would indeed beget many children; he would become wealthy and powerful. But he would never attain the interior harmony that is crucial to the truly blessed life. As a result, perhaps, his God seemed remote. The sense of transcendence and of the sacred dimension of life, which was an essential part of blessing, was evidently linked to the integrity of a life that has come to terms with the past and with the demands of the intractable self.

When God had summoned Abraham, he had commanded him to leave everything behind and to press forward toward the unknown and the future. He had encouraged the patriarch to cut himself off ruthlessly from anything that might impede his progress. Unwelcome realities were to be dispatched to the desert. But while this absolutism might be necessary for certain pioneers, it could lead to a lack of pity and compassion. It was also, in the end, counterproductive. The sons whom Abraham sent to the godless realm of the east became the progenitors of nations that would be very troublesome to Israel in the future. At Bethel, however, God introduced a new dynamic into the religious life of Israel. Jacob must one day return to the Promised Land. Uncomfortable realities would not go away. Not only must Jacob go back to the land of the Promise but he must also at some point make peace with Esau. Instead of cutting himself off from the past, Jacob had as his ultimate duty to become reconciled with it. Jacob would remain in Mesopotamia for twenty years, but he was always aware of the wrong he had done his brother. In wounding Esau he had also inflicted a wound on his own soul, and this fissure must be healed before Jacob could enjoy the true fruitfulness and harmony of blessing.

A Blessing or a Curse?

FOR TWENTY YEARS, JACOB LIVED IN THE household of his wily uncle Laban in Paddan-Aram, Mesopotamia. Power should radiate from a man who is filled with blessing, so that everything with which he comes in contact prospers. And in some respects, Jacob did prove to be a source of blessing to Laban and his family. We have seen that blessing liberates the creativity which is the source of wealth; blessing enables a human being to operate productively in the world. Even Laban, who exploited and tricked Jacob for years, was ready to admit that "the Lord has blessed me because of you" (30:27). His wealth had increased. Jacob reminds him, "For you had little before I came, and it has increased abundantly; and the Lord has blessed you wherever I turned" (30:30).

But the conflict within Jacob's soul made it impossible for him to achieve a harmonious family life. He had fallen instantly in love with Rachel, Laban's beautiful younger daughter, and since he had arrived penniless in Paddan-Aram, he had to work for Laban for seven years to win her hand. But on the wedding night, Laban sent his older daughter Leah into Jacob's bed in Rachel's stead. In the blindness of night, Jacob found himself in the same position as his father. Even though he claimed to love Rachel with all his heart, he mistook her for her sister. "When morning came," says the narrator wryly, "it was Leah!" (29:25). When he confronted Laban, his uncle blandly informed him: "This is not done in our country—giving the younger before the firstborn" (29:26). Jacob the trickster had been duped in his turn. With strong poetic irony, he was forced to acknowledge the rights of the firstborn child. Before he was given Rachel in marriage too, he had to agree to work for Laban for another seven years. But his marriage to the sisters did not bring peace to the household. Because Jacob loved Rachel and not Leah, he introduced the same sibling rivalry into Laban's home that had split his own family asunder.

There was cruelty in Jacob. He was never able to forgive Leah for Laban's trick. Perhaps, as the elder sibling, she reminded him too strongly of the wrong he had done to Esau. He made it absolutely clear to Leah that she was unloved. Yet again, Genesis reminds us of the unfairness of love and of the inconsolable pain of the rejected. God tried to make things up to Leah. Like the other matriarchs of Israel, Rachel proved to be barren, her sterility a reminder of the continuing difficulty of implementing the divine blessing in our world. But the despised Leah was, indirectly, blessed by God. She alone proved to be fertile, able to conceive easily and give Jacob one son after another.

Yet we see the depth of Leah's pain in the names she gave her children. When Reuben ("Behold a Son!") was born, her triumph was mingled with bitterness and a forlorn hope. "Because the Lord has looked on my affliction," she said, "surely now my husband will love me" (29:32). Each time she conceived, she nurtured the same yearning, but always in vain. When she gave birth to Simeon ("Hearing"), she said, "Because the Lord has heard that I am hated, he has given me this son also" (29:33). Her third son was named Levi ("Joining") because, she hoped, "Now this time my husband will be joined to me, because I have borne him three sons" (28:34). But Jacob continued to despise Leah. It seemed impossible for humanity, in its exile from Eden, to enjoy unmixed blessing. Leah was the only matriarch to enjoy the fecundity of the Promise, but Jacob's neglect poisoned her life and retarded her development. Momentarily, however, when her fourth son, Judah ("Giving Thanks"), arrived, Leah seemed able to make an effort to transcend her distress, saying simply, "This time I will praise the Lord" (29:35). Perhaps for that reason, Judah would eventually be able to overcome the hatred tearing at his family and become a source of blessing and reconciliation.

But the strife between Rachel and Leah was not over. If Leah was impoverished and belittled by the lack of love, Rachel experienced her barrenness as a curse which soured her relationship with her husband and her God. Instead of entreating Yahweh for children, she turned on Jacob. "Give me children," she cried explosively, "or I shall die!" (30:1). Again, instead of reasoning kindly with her, Jacob raged back: "Am I in the place of God, who has withheld from you the fruit of the womb?" (30:2). This was no marriage made in heaven. Emulating Sarah, Rachel gave her husband her servant Bilhah to bear children on her behalf—a solution which we have seen to be itself a potential source of strife. Bilhah bore Jacob two sons, and Leah, who had temporarily stopped conceiving, responded by giving Jacob *her* servant Zilpah, who also gave birth to two sons. The atmosphere in the household was electric with tension and jealousy as the two sisters crowed triumphantly over each other as each successive son was born. When Bilhah gave birth to Dan ("He Has Done Justice"), Rachel cried, "God has judged me, and has also heard my voice and given me a son" (30:6). Rachel did not see the birth of children as a God-given blessing but as something that was her due. Bilhah's fertility had been subsumed into her own private fight with Leah. When Bilhah bore Naphtali ("My Struggle"), Rachel proudly announced, "With mighty wrestlings I have wrestled with my sister, and have prevailed" (30:8). Leah herself could not contain her triumph when Zilpah added sons to *her* camp. "Good fortune [*gad*]!" she exulted when Gad was born; when Asher ("Happiness") arrived, she continued to preen herself: "Happy am I! For the women will call me happy" (30:11, 13). Her pride knew no bounds when she bore two more sons of her own. God seemed to have rewarded her for giving Zilpah to Jacob, so she called her new baby Issachar ("There Is Hire"), and when her last son was born, she confidently called him Zebulon ("Prince"). But she still craved love. "God has endowed me with a good dowry," she said hopefully. "Now my husband will honor me, because I have borne him six sons" (30:20). But again, her hope was frustrated. Her next child was a mere girl, whose birth was a nonevent and was greeted with no exclamation of any kind. We shall see that Jacob disliked Dinah all her life, simply because she was Leah's daughter.

Jacob's hatred of Leah sprang from the split in his own soul. Throughout Genesis, we have seen that human beings tend to project their guilt outward when in the wrong. Adam, Eve, and Noah had all turned viciously on others when they had sinned. Jacob had made Leah a scapegoat for his treatment of Esau and had become a curse and impediment to her. Because she was so obviously despised by her husband, Leah's joy in her blessed fertility was never unalloyed. She was never able to grow and fulfill her potential in motherhood, but was always held back by bitterness and sorrow. The jealousy and strife that Jacob's unequal treatment of the two sisters had planted in his family spread to the children. The anger and rivalry expressed in the names of his sons showed that the conflict and hatred were etched deeply into their identity. They began early to take sides in the struggle between the two wives, as we see when Reuben, Leah's oldest son, brought mandrakes to his mother to act as an aphrodisiac. The blessing of fertility and love had become a source of discord and barren competition. This family hatred would erupt in fearful, murderous violence. Eventually, God took pity on Rachel and allowed her to conceive a child of her own. But even Rachel, the beloved wife, was impaired by the psychic pain suffered by all the members of Jacob's family. When Joseph was born, instead of being overcome with joy and gratitude, Rachel simply demanded more. "God has taken away (*asaf*) my reproach," she said. "May the Lord add (*yosef*) to me another son!" (30:23–24). She too had been damaged and frustrated by the years of sterility and strife. Her focus was herself: like a cursed person, she was unable to achieve self-transcendence. Jacob would love Joseph as unfairly as he would despise Dinah, simply because he was the child of the beloved Rachel. This would plant new seeds of rage and jealousy in this most unhappy family.

Jacob Agonistes

 THERE COULD BE NO PEACE FOR JACOB OR HIS family until he had finally confronted his past and achieved a reconciliation with Esau. This demanded a mighty psychic struggle. The birth of Joseph to the beloved Rachel seemed to convince Jacob that a chapter in his life had ended. The joy of this unexpected addition to the family may also have given him the courage he needed to return home. He did not leave Paddan-Aram, however, without tricking Laban out of the best of his flock by means of a clever ruse. As a result of this sharp practice, Jacob "grew exceedingly rich, and had large flocks, and male and female slaves, and camels and donkeys" (30:43). Jacob was able to achieve the outer marks of a blessed life but not the interior harmony and liberation of blessing, and this failure vitiated the rest. His abundant progeny had been conceived in an atmosphere of hatred, and his wealth achieved by the guile of the serpent. The text goes out of its way to emphasize the nefarious aspect of Jacob's character at this point. In this respect, at least, Rachel and Jacob were well matched. When they finally left Laban's household and began their journey to Canaan, she had stolen Laban's household gods just as, twenty years earlier, Jacob had stolen his father's blessing.

Ultimately, it is neither riches nor offspring which yield a sense of the divine but the attempt to integrate the inner self. This became clear as Jacob approached his homeland and experienced a theophany on the borders of Canaan. In Mesopotamia he had experienced no clear vision of his God, though he believed that God was with him. He had sometimes interpreted a bright (and dubious) idea of his own, such as the duping of Laban, as a divine inspiration (31:9–13). He had felt a sacred power at work in the complexities of his own nature: God had been present in Jacob's "subtle," serpentine ideas, as well as in his more conventionally pious decisions. But as he drew near to Canaan, the land of his destiny, he realized that he had entered quite a different realm of religious experience: "Jacob went on his way and the angels of God met him; and when Jacob saw them he said, 'This is God's camp!' So he called that place Mahanaim

["Double Camp"]" (32:1–2). Life immediately assumed a "double" aspect; each apparently mundane event would also have a divine dimension. God sent messengers to Jacob, and he responded by dispatching messengers to his brother Esau. Already Jacob had sensed that in addressing his brother, he was in some mysterious sense appealing to his God. For twenty years, Jacob had agonized over Esau, and his message was uncharacteristically pleading and sycophantic:

> "Thus says your servant Jacob, 'I have lived with Laban as an alien, and stayed until now; and I have oxen, donkeys, flocks, male and female slaves; and I have sent to tell my lord, in order that I might find favor in your sight.' " (32:4–5)

His messengers returned with the fearful news that Esau was already on his way to Jacob—at the head of four hundred fighting men.

Jacob immediately assumed the worst. In fear and distress, he divided his followers into two camps in the hope that some of them might escape his brother's onslaught. Then he took refuge with his God. No longer confident of his own cleverness and subtlety, he felt unworthy, too small for the divine blessing which had enabled him to return to Canaan a rich man. Yet he realized that he must go forward to confront the past; he had to come to terms with the complexities of his youth in a way that his father, Isaac, for example, had never done. Jacob was the first of the patriarchs to make a return journey. Henceforth the whole notion of return would become an important symbol of integration and reconciliation in the faith of Israel. It was no longer sufficient to "get up and go." The patriarchs had to learn that no one could move forward creatively into the future without having made peace with the past.

The next day, Jacob dispatched a huge gift of livestock to his brother: goats, sheep, camels, cows, bulls, and donkeys. His envoys were to tell Esau that "your servant Jacob" was behind them (32:18, 20). Jacob obviously wanted to appease his brother, but he was, at least subconsciously, aware that at Mahanaim, everything had a double aspect, human and divine. The New Revised Standard Version translates Jacob's thought economically: "Afterwards I shall see his face; perhaps he will accept me" (32:20). But Everett Fox has preserved the insistent diction of the Hebrew, which forces the reader to look forward to the imminent divine wrestling match at Peniel, when Jacob would see his God "face to face" (32:30).

> For [Jacob] said to himself:
> I will wipe [the anger from] his face
> with the gift that goes ahead of my face;
> afterward, when I see his face,
> perhaps he will lift up my face.[12]

The text is subtly directing our attention to the fact that the "face" of God and the "faces" of Jacob and Esau are all one and the same. By facing his brother, Jacob would confront the "face" of his God; but he would also confront himself. Jacob was having to come to terms not only with his wronged brother, but with the "Esau" within. Jacob had to engage with the alter ego that he hated and had tried to discard. Only when he confronted those aspects of his personality that filled him with fear and disgust—the polar opposite of his waking self—could he heal the conflict in his soul and experience the healing power of the divine.

We have already seen what happened next at the Jabbok ford, at the place which Jacob renamed Peniel, "Face of God." A mysterious stranger came to him during the night and wrestled with him all night long. At the end of the match, Jacob became aware that he had been fighting with his God. Where Abraham had cordially entertained a stranger who turned out to be Yahweh, Jacob, a more conflicted character, had to struggle with his divine assailant. No two people will experience the divine in the same way. The antagonistic embrace of the wrestler mirrored, perhaps, the conflict of Jacob's own marital embrace. Psychologists speak of the "dream work" that we all accomplish at night at some profound level of our being, which enables us to look at issues that our conscious, daytime self finds impossible to face. Perhaps in some deep reach of his memory, Jacob recalled his wrestling match with Esau in the womb, as he internally prepared for his meeting with his brother in the morning. When he woke, he felt profoundly "blessed," and empowered. Transformed and enlightened by his encounter with a power which he had experienced as divine, Jacob set off at daybreak to meet Esau face to face.

Immediately he saw Esau and his fighting men approaching. Jacob may have been strengthened by his psychic combat, but he was not an entirely reformed character. Showing the blatant favoritism which had soured his family life and would be the cause of much future unhappiness, Jacob positioned his concubines Bilhah and Zilpah with their sons at the head of his procession, in the most dangerous position; Leah and her children came next; finally, Rachel and Joseph brought up the rear. Jacob himself walked ahead of his family, but, in an astonishing reversal of our expectations, Esau "ran to meet him, and embraced him, and fell on his neck and kissed him, and they wept" (33:4). Esau had always been consumed by the passion of the moment, incapable either of foresight or of brooding on the past. He was amazed that Jacob should have thought the lavish gifts to be necessary. But Jacob recognized that this extraordinary reconciliation had sacred significance. "No, please; if I find favor with you, then accept my present from my hand; for truly to see your face is like seeing the face of God—since you have received me with such favor" (33:10).

It is as though, for a fleeting moment, the warring sides of Jacob's divided self had come together. The brothers were total opposites: Jacob all shrewd calculation and Esau, incapable of reflection or of nursing a grudge, instinctively impelled into the arms of his brother. The unexpected union was an experience of such harmony and wholeness that it shocked Esau into tears and forced even the wary Jacob to sense it as a theophany. Yet it was not a moment of conversion. As we shall see, Jacob proved incapable of applying this experience to the rest of his life. The Hebrew Bible does not offer us happy endings, as we shall find after another tearful reconciliation scene at the very end of Genesis.

Once Jacob had arrived back in Canaan, God confirmed the Promise. Jacob would indeed be the father of a mighty nation, and the land of Canaan would be given to his descendants. "Then," the narrator continued, "God went up from him" (35:9–13). Jacob experienced no more theophanies. Indeed, God would make no further appearance in Genesis. He seems to have decided to withdraw from the human stage; this marked another crucial phase in the gradual separation of God and humanity which has been increasing throughout Genesis. Henceforth, Jacob and his family would be forced to rely on their own ideas, dreams, and intuitions, without explicit divine instruction. God would remain hidden, directing events from behind the scenes. When he next makes an appearance, in the Book of Exodus, God is a more untouchable being. He would not think of appearing in human form or sitting with his chosen ones as a friend. The God of Moses insists on his separation from the mundane; human beings must keep their distance and appreciate God's essential otherness or "holiness." But in the course of Genesis, God had made it clear how people should experience the divine. Human beings were indeed to be one another's keeper; they would be able to sense life's sacred dimension when they displayed practical compassion toward their fellow men and women and when they wrestled manfully with the turbulent, conflicted world of the psyche.

The Rape of Dinah

 JACOB NEVER SEEMED TO ABSORB THIS LESson. After his superb moment at Peniel, when he did indeed achieve a momentary self-transcendence, he appeared to fall into a state of chronic egotism and self-indulgence. This became horribly apparent in Chapter 34. Jacob had settled opposite the city of Shechem, in the northern highlands of Canaan. One day his daughter Dinah was brutally raped by a young man, also called Shechem, the son of Hamor, the Hivite chieftain of the region. Dinah was kept in the city as a hostage, but Shechem, the rapist, fell passionately in love with her and instructed his father to procure her for him in marriage.

At the time of the rape, Jacob's sons were away from home with their flocks. But Jacob was in the family encampment outside the town. His reaction was chilling. He had "heard that Shechem had defiled his daughter Dinah," the narrator tells us, but "held his peace" awaiting the return of his sons (34:5). Jacob was not a restrained man. We shall see that when another of his children met with disaster, he was inconsolable. But this time he simply "held his peace"—*hekharish,* a word that in the Bible usually connotes culpable inertia or negligence.[13] He made no attempt to rescue his daughter from the town, and did not even bother to summon his sons home. The narrator gives us a clue to Jacob's extraordinary apathy at the very beginning of the chapter, when he reminds us that Dinah was Jacob's daughter by Leah.

Jacob's callous indifference is all the more shocking when we compare him with Hamor the Hivite, who was ready to stop at nothing to secure the happiness and well-being of *his* child. He begged Jacob to allow Dinah to marry Shechem, declaring that Jacob could ask as high a dowry as he chose. Equally telling was the outrage of Jacob's sons when they came home and heard what had happened to their sister. The narrator informs us first that they were grieved for Dinah; only after that does he say that they were also enraged. The pain and sympathy they felt for their wronged sister were stronger than their anger. They were also horrified. This rape of Israel's daughter was "an outrage," "a thing [that] ought not to be done" (34:7). Yet still Jacob remained silent and took no part at all in the brothers' attempt to rescue Dinah.

The brothers had clearly inherited Jacob's guile. They told Hamor and Shechem that it would be dishonorable for their sister to marry an uncircumcised man. If the local Hivites were willing to be circumcised, they would be glad to intermarry with them. Astonishingly, Hamor persuaded all the men of the city of Shechem to undergo the ordeal of circumcision, though the text makes it clear that financial and practical considerations were a powerful incentive. Jacob was a rich man, and it would obviously be advantageous for the Hivites to engage in trade with his family. All the males were circumcised, and three days after the operation, when they were still weak and in pain, Simeon and Levi, Dinah's brothers, entered the city and slaughtered them all. Then they rescued their sister. After they had left the town and returned to Jacob's camp, the other brothers arrived. Like scavenging wild beasts, they

> came upon the slain, and plundered the city, because their sister had been defiled. They took their flocks and their herds, their donkeys, and whatever was in the city and in the field. All their wealth, all their little ones and their wives, all that was in the houses, they captured and made their prey. (34:27–29)

Until this point, the narrator has been sympathetic to Dinah's brothers, but he does not flinch from exposing the full horror and cold-blooded violence of their crime. Abraham and Isaac had both lived on good terms with the native people of Canaan. This episode opened a new chapter of distrust, hatred, and contempt. This was just the first of many Israelite massacres of the indigenous population of the Promised Land. Coming so soon after the reconciliation scene between Jacob and Esau, it shatters all our hopes of peace and harmony. A "terror from God" struck the towns in the region after the slaughter, so that nobody dared to pursue the sons of Jacob (35:5).

Like so many of the stories of Genesis, this is no straightforward tale of right and wrong. The text emphasizes the brutality of the rape, which reduced Dinah to a mere object: we are told that Shechem "lay with her by force" (34:2) rather than the usual phrase "lay with her." We are also shocked by the Hivites' insouciance afterward. They cheerfully proposed intermarriage and trade agreements as though nothing had happened. Simeon and Levi's massacre is utterly abhorrent, the first major crime of the people of Israel. But at least they left the city as soon as they had fought their way through to Dinah. The narrator gives the impression that the looting of the other brothers was even more repellent, because simply venal. There are no heroes in this sorry tale; all are villains—with the obvious exception of poor Dinah. Yet, in the end, Jacob emerged as the most culpable character in the story.

At last, at the end of the massacre and the plunder, Jacob broke his long, shameful silence. Did he express horror at the cruelty of the crime? Did he finally lament the outrage suffered by his daughter? Did he grieve for the slain? Apparently, these considerations weighed little with the patriarch of Israel. He simply regretted the danger that Simeon and Levi had brought upon the family and—above all—upon himself:

> "You have brought trouble on me by making me odious to the inhabitants of the land, the Canaanites and the Perizzites; my numbers are few, and if they gather themselves against me and attack me, I shall be destroyed, both me and my household." (34:30)

The inadequacy of this response is one of the most shocking moments in a shocking story. It is as odious as his initial indifference to Dinah's plight. Much of this catastrophe must be laid at Jacob's door. We recall that the very names of Simeon and Levi expressed the pain of their unloved mother. Tension and resentment had so divided the family that the brothers would naturally be inclined to overreact to an injury committed against their slighted sister. The violence that erupted so viciously at Shechem had incubated for years in the seething hatred and envy of Jacob's household. As if to point to Jacob's culpability, Simeon and Levi are given the last, devastating word. After Jacob's rebuke, the brothers point out that it was Dinah's rape that was the cause of their crime, a fact that Jacob had managed to ignore completely in his puling self-pity. "Should our sister be treated like a whore?" they ask defiantly (34:31). But they are also implying that Jacob himself had treated Dinah as a prostitute: by doing nothing, he had tacitly suggested that the rape of his daughter was acceptable to him.

The Fall of Jacob

JACOB'S RETURN TO THE PROMISED LAND had begun so well. He had confronted his inner demons at the ford of Jabbok, made peace with his brother, and achieved thereby an extraordinary moment of intimacy with his God. He was confirmed as the true son of the Promise. Yet he seemed unable—or perhaps he was merely unwilling—to allow these profound experiences to transform his behavior. All the great world religions insist that vision and ecstasy can never be ends in themselves. The test of true spirituality is that it be successfully integrated with the rest of life. The word "ecstasy" means a going forth from the self. It is the corollary of blessing, which enables a person to break the imprisoning boundaries of space, time, and the ego to achieve an enhanced, liberated life. Jacob was unable to take the final step to wholeness. After his return from Mesopotamia, he remained the heir of the Promise but was rarely a blessing to the people around him. Destruction, not benediction, emanated from Jacob. Like a man accursed, he began to blight his surroundings, and as the rape of Dinah shows, he was a source of death and discord instead of life and harmony. The story indicates that Jacob had, after all, not been able to come to terms with Esau and all that his brother represented. His guilt and fear of Esau had poisoned his relationship with Leah, and that, in turn, had eaten away at the rest of the family. After his return to Canaan, moreover, his treatment of Dinah suggests that his old trouble had assumed chronic proportions. His whining self-pity and self-indulgence would also increase with age. Instead of achieving liberation from the ego and past resentment, Jacob had become their prisoner.

Death and violence continued to radiate from Jacob, the center of the family circle. Rachel had become pregnant once again, but this blessing turned into a curse when she died in labor. Jacob had clearly learned nothing about the dangers of favoritism and named her second son Benjamin, "Child of My Right Hand." Immediately afterward, we are told, Reuben, Leah's eldest son, made an attempt to assert his position as Jacob's firstborn. He, not Benjamin, should be the child of his father's right hand. Accordingly, Reuben had intercourse with his father's concubine Bilhah, Rachel's handmaid, an act of posthumous aggression against her dead mistress. It was also an act with dynastic implications, since it symbolically represented the son's taking his father's place. Centuries later, King David's son Absalom made a point of sleeping with his father's concubines when he was attempting to usurp the throne.[14] Reuben's ploy, however, did not succeed. The narrator concludes the episode with the terse comment "and Israel heard of it" (35:22). This can hardly have improved the atmosphere in this hate-ridden family.

Next we read of the death of Isaac, who had, apparently, lingered on his deathbed for twenty years, blind, feeble, and immobile—a graphic image of the decline of the patriarchate. After their father's death, Esau and Jacob parted company. The narrator tries to give the impression that it was an amicable separation, explaining that the twins were too rich to share the same territory. But Esau's departure to Seir, the mountainous region to the southeast of Canaan, shows that the emotional reconciliation of the brothers had come to nothing. Jacob could live neither with his brother nor with his own shadow self. He did not achieve the psychic healing of blessing. This marked the beginning of a long political conflict, as with Abraham's discarded sons whose descendants became the enemies of Israel. The narrator tells us that "Esau is Edom" (36:8); Edom was a kingdom that became a bitter rival to Israel at the time of King David.

Joseph

 AS SOON AS JOSEPH IS BORN, THE READER expects him to be important. Rachel gave birth to him with great difficulty and after years of barrenness, and in Genesis the chosen one is usually born to a hitherto sterile woman. We are not surprised that the last portion of the book includes a novella describing Joseph's career. Maybe he would bring new hope to Jacob's troubled family? Yet the first thing we learn about Joseph is disturbing. After spending time in the field with his brothers, the seventeen-year-old boy "brought a bad report of them to their father" (37:2). Nobody likes a sneak, and Joseph is unlikely to thrive amid the tensions of this family. Next we find that Jacob was still indulging his preference for Rachel and her children and that this favoritism had the usual destructive results:

> Now Israel [Jacob] loved Joseph more than any other of his children, because he was the son of his old age; and he had made him a long robe with sleeves. But when his brothers saw that their father loved

him more than all his brothers, they hated him, and could not speak peaceably to him. (37:3–4)

Joseph then compounded the already dangerous situation by bragging about his dreams. He told his brothers that he had seen their sheaves of corn bowing down before him; even the sun, moon, and stars had prostrated themselves before him. "Are you indeed to reign over us? Are you indeed to have dominion over us?" demanded his brothers, the Hebrew stuttering with fury. "So they hated him even more because of his dreams and his words" (37:8). Even his doting father rebuked Joseph for his presumption, but, the narrator tells us, he kept Joseph's words in mind and pondered them secretly.

Jacob had himself been a dreamer, glimpsing on two occasions the sacred dimension of the mundane world. In the Bible, dreams are usually a revelation of a divinely perceived reality or of future events, rather than an expression of the dreamer's internal state. Jacob would naturally have regarded his beloved son's dreams as a sign of divine election. Nevertheless, there is something disturbing about these dreams. Jacob's dreams had in the main focused upon God, but God did not appear in any of Joseph's dreams. Joseph's dreams were a prediction of the future, but they also centered somewhat obsessively on himself. Joseph had believed from the outset that he was born to greatness, and he continued throughout his life to assume that he was unquestionably the leading character in the scenario that unfolded around him and that he was directing events.

God never spoke to Joseph directly. He had vanished from the human scene. Like us, Joseph had to work without divine guidance, his data frequently perplexing and ambiguous. He had to find an interpretation for his dreams himself. He received privileged information about the future but had clearly not yet received enlightenment. His unpleasant boasting about his nocturnal visions revealed that he was totally lacking in sensitivity and in wisdom about how best to deal with an increasingly dangerous situation. In the way he recounted his dreams, we sense a yearning for quasi-divine status that reminds us uneasily of Adam and Eve and the builders of Babel. He had provoked his brothers and exploited his special position in the family, and so was in part the author of his own imminent misfortunes. The situation looks bleak indeed. Nevertheless, the whole family, which seemed so lost to hatred, resentment, and egotism, was about to begin a painful journey to self-knowledge that would bring them, at last, a measure of peace.

We have already seen that, when pushed, the brothers resorted easily to violence. They resolved to get rid of Joseph and seized the opportunity to do so when they were tending the flocks, far from home. They decided to throw him into a pit and tell their father that he had been eaten by a wild animal. The text is confused. The editors probably combined two versions of the story but have used this ambiguity to introduce us to Judah, the fourth son of Leah, who would play an increasingly important part in the drama. In one version, Reuben tried to save Joseph's life and appeared in the guise of the "good brother." He urged his brothers not to kill Joseph but to throw him into the pit, intending to return later to rescue him. We have just seen Reuben trying to assert his position as the firstborn and failing grotesquely. Was this an attempt to reinstate himself with his father? The other version makes Judah the one to modify the plan. At this point, Judah is still a lost soul, angling for position. Simeon and Levi had irreparably discredited themselves with Jacob by their part in the Shechem massacre, and Judah was next in line. He may have felt that Jacob's obvious preference for Joseph could endanger his own position. Judah suggested that they sell Joseph to some passing Arab merchants. He wanted to cash in on Joseph's removal from the family scene.

The narrator reports the ensuing events with terrible simplicity. The brothers pulled off Joseph's robe, "the long robe with sleeves that he wore; and they took him and threw him into a pit. The pit was empty; there was no water in it. They then sat down to eat" (37:23–25). They could clearly be just as callous and indifferent to human suffering as their father. The text gives two contradictory accounts of what happened next. Did the brothers sell Joseph to some passing Arab traders? Or did some passing Midianites pull Joseph out of the pit and sell him to the Arabs? At all events, when Reuben returned later to rescue Joseph, he found that the pit was empty. Tearing his clothes as a sign of mourning, he returned to his brothers. "The boy has gone," he said, "and I, where can I turn?" (37:30). Impotently wringing his hands and without direction, Reuben appears as a man wholly lost to blessing and unable to function effectively, despite his good intentions.

The text tells us nothing at this point about Joseph's reactions. It is only later that we learn of his "anguish" and that he "pleaded" with his obdurate brothers (42:21). All his grandiose visions of future glory fell away. The boy who had dreamed of domination had to descend into the pit, not knowing whether he would live or die. For the first time, we feel sympathy for Joseph. Henceforth, like his father, he would have to struggle to survive. His expectation of a glittering future gave him no confidence at this fearful moment. As so often in myth and legend, the hero can achieve enlightenment only by taking an arduous path through the shadow of death. Joseph experienced real desolation; faith does not insulate the characters of the Bible from the terrors of the human condition.

Meanwhile the brothers had broken the news to Jacob. Dipping Joseph's elaborate tunic in the blood of a goat, they told him: "This we have found; see now whether it is your son's robe or not" (37:32). Jacob, who had himself deceived his father, was now deceived by his own sons. Like Isaac, he was now too spiritually blind to recognize the truth, even though, as we shall see, he nurtured a subconscious suspicion. The truth would throw too harsh a light on his own parental deficiency. Instead Jacob gazed at the bloody tunic and said, "A wild animal has devoured him; Joseph is without doubt torn to pieces" (37:33). Such a tragic death for Joseph was terrible, but preferable to the hideous notion that his own blind favoritism had made fratricides of his sons. He then succumbed completely and self-indulgently to his grief: "All his sons and all his daughters sought to comfort him; but he refused to be comforted, and said, 'No, I shall go down to Sheol to my son, mourning'" (37:35). Jacob's extravagant mourning was a cruel demonstration to his remaining children that they were totally irrelevant to him. Without Joseph, life was not worth living.

Judah and Tamar

 AT THIS POINT, THE EDITORS HAVE INSERTED a tale that seems out of place. We are forced to leave Joseph and Jacob and enter the family of Judah. Recently, however, commentators have shown that the story is deeply linked to what has gone before. Like his brothers, Judah had stood silently by and watched his father grieve for Joseph. Then he himself had to learn what it was like to lose, not one son, but two. Er, his firstborn, died—killed by God, the author tells us cryptically. It was then the duty of Judah's second son, Onan, to have intercourse with Er's wife, Tamar, to give her a child in his brother's name and so continue his brother's line. But Onan selfishly refused to carry out this fraternal obligation, apparently content that the lives of Er and Tamar should lack meaning and end in nothingness. So God killed Onan too. Tamar thus seemed to bring bad luck, and Judah would not permit his only surviving son, Shelah, to marry her when he came of age. Tamar got her revenge. She refused to allow her life to finish in a void. She therefore disguised herself as a prostitute and tricked Judah into having sex with her. Three months later, when Judah learned that his daughter-in-law was pregnant, he brusquely ordered her to be burned alive. But Tamar sent him the signet, cord, and staff she had taken from Judah as a pledge when they had intercourse. "Take note, please, whose these are," she said, using the same Hebrew phrase the brothers had used when they presented Joseph's bloodstained tunic to Jacob. Unlike his father, however, Judah allowed himself to perceive the truth. "She is more in the right than I," he admitted, "since I did not give her to my son Shelah" (38:25–26).

Judah had begun the painful journey from selfishness and ignorance to self-knowledge. He had also learned that it is impossible to save what we love by holding on to it, in defiance of what we know to be right. Tamar gave birth to twins: Perez and Zerah, two sons to replace the children Judah had lost. Again, a woman had to step in when the men of the family had lost their way. Like Rebekah, Tamar was forced to a desperate expedient to ensure that God's will was done. Perez would be the ancestor of the great King David.

Joseph in Egypt

 MEANWHILE, JOSEPH HAD BEEN TAKEN BY the Arab merchants to Egypt and sold to Potiphar, one of Pharaoh's officials and a commander in the Egyptian army. In exile from his family, Joseph became a man of ability and stature. He rose to a privileged position in Potiphar's household and proved that he had sound moral principles when he resisted the blandishments of Potiphar's wife. He also had stamina; when Potiphar's scorned wife had him thrown into prison, Joseph did not repine, gained the confidence of his warders, and finally was able to extricate himself by his adroit interpretation of Pharaoh's dreams. He became grand vizier of Egypt. Joseph was a survivor who, unlike Noah and Lot, used his experience to find some measure of healing. The naming of children is important in Genesis; it can be a useful indication of a person's state of mind. When Joseph's two sons were born, he did not give vent to the bitterness and rage that he must have felt toward his brothers. Instead, he seemed able to use his present good fortune to assuage the sufferings of the past:

> Joseph named the firstborn Manasseh ["He Who Makes Me Forget"], "For," he said, "God has made me forget all my hardship and all my father's house." The second he named Ephraim ["Double Fruit"], "For God has made me fruitful in the land of my misfortunes." (41:51–52)

But it is never safe to assume that we have wholly transcended past pain and resentment. Joseph had not completely forgotten, as events would prove. He had achieved some measure of insight, but had repressed a good deal. He had not yet attained the plateau of serenity that he claimed. Nor had he entirely overcome the arrogance and other less pleasing traits he had acquired in his father's household.

This became clear when the famine that Joseph had foretold struck Egypt and the surrounding countries. As vizier, Joseph had carefully prepared and provisioned the country, and now people from the adjacent lands flocked there for supplies. Canaan had been grievously afflicted, and Jacob dispatched his sons to buy food in Egypt. Still blindly partial to Rachel's children, he kept Benjamin with him at home.

Recognition

 AND SO IT WAS THAT THE TEN BROTHERS came into the presence of Joseph. Ever since Isaac mistook Jacob for his beloved Esau, the ability to recognize a person or an object has been an indication of a person's spiritual insight and capacity for painful truth. Joseph and his brothers not only had to recognize one another but they also had to acknowledge the pain and conflict within. Joseph had the advantage: he "recognized his brothers, [but] they did not recognize him" (42:8). As soon as they came before this powerful man, the ten brothers "bowed themselves before him with their faces to the ground" (42:6). They had unwit-

tingly fulfilled the dream of the young Joseph, performing an obeisance that once seemed unthinkable.

Not surprisingly, the irony was not lost on Joseph, who now
"remembered the dreams that he had dreamed about them" (42:9).
Hitherto, the revelations of his dreams had been directed toward the
future; now the memory of his dreams forced him to look back to
the past. He obviously felt more ambivalence and anger than he had
realized, because he suddenly lashed out at his unsuspecting brothers and accused them of espionage: "You are spies," he said, "you
have come to see the nakedness of the land!" (42:9). It was a strange
charge. Was Joseph merely motivated by revenge? Was he, naturally
enough, unable to view his brethren with anything but mistrust,
which made the notion of treachery spring instantly to mind?
Almost certainly, his mind was flooded with the memories of that
past betrayal. The phrase "the nakedness of the land" reminds us
how frequently sexuality had been linked to cruelty and violence in
Jacob's family. The phrase also reminds us of the naked vulnerability of Adam and Eve after their sin. Perhaps the shock of seeing his
brothers brought back to Joseph his terrible impotence the last time
he had seen them, when they threw him into the pit. How would
this family ever manage to redeem the past?

The brothers were stunned by Joseph's accusations. They
embarked on a series of explanations which show that even though
they had not yet recognized Joseph, there was something about the
grand vizier that brought their lost brother to the edge of their consciousness. "We are all [emphasis added] sons of one man; . . . . the
youngest, however, is now with our father, and one is no more"
(42:11, 13). This excursus into family history was neither necessary
nor relevant to the charge of spying, but perhaps the accusation of
treachery had stirred uneasy memories of their past crime. The

brothers were on the brink of recognizing the full significance of their past actions.

Joseph was clearly worried by this mention of Benjamin. How could he leave Rachel's other child in the hands of these would-be fratricides? But he proceeded carefully. First he threw his brothers into prison and let them stew there for three days. He had set himself up as therapist, as it were, and was about to force them to confront their guilt. By making them experience some of his own past sufferings, he hoped to make them acknowledge their own cruelty. Three days later, Joseph announced that he would take Simeon as a hostage but would release the rest, on condition that they returned to Egypt, bringing Benjamin back with them. By this time, his treatment had begun to work. The brothers had started to talk compulsively about Joseph, their lost brother. "Alas, we are paying the penalty for what we did to our brother," they said. "We saw his anguish when he pleaded with us, but we would not listen. That is why this anguish has come upon us" (42:21). Instead of seeing Joseph as an object of hatred, they were beginning to empathize with his pain and take it into themselves.

When Joseph overheard this, the narrator tells us, "he turned away from them and wept" (42:24). It was some time before he was able to speak. It is a revelation to us—and was, perhaps, to him—of his vulnerability. This unexpected meeting stirred up feelings that he imagined he had forgotten, and the pain that he had suppressed began to rise to the surface. His tears show that he had a depth of feeling that we have not seen hitherto. He had hoped to effect a change of heart in his brothers, but now we see that he was beginning to be transformed himself.

When the brothers returned to Canaan, Joseph had arranged for the money they had brought to buy food to be concealed in their bags. When they found it, they were filled with panic, guilt, and a sense of foreboding. For the first time, they mentioned God. The painful confrontation with the past and the stirrings of new sympathy had made them aware of life's mystery and pain. When they stood before their father, explained Simeon's absence, and told him the whole story, Jacob's own memory was quickened. He recalled the last time they had reported the loss of a brother, and though Simeon's loss was not the brothers' fault, he turned on them with an accusation. "I am the one you have bereaved of children," he cried. "Joseph is no more, and Simeon is no more, and now you would take Benjamin" (42:36). The veiled accusation suggests that Jacob may long have harbored buried suspicions about Joseph's disappearance and his brothers' part in the tragedy. Yet his response was typically maudlin and self-pitying. "All this has happened to me!" he complained; when he contemplated the possible loss of Benjamin, he yet again discounted the children that remained to him. As far as Jacob was concerned, Benjamin "alone is left"; if he lost Benjamin too, he told his sons, "you would bring down my gray hairs with sorrow to Sheol" (42:38).

Judah's Intervention

 BUT THE FAMINE GOT WORSE, AND IT WAS clear that if the clan was to survive, the brothers would have to return to Egypt for supplies. It was Judah who was able to persuade his father that he must risk losing Benjamin in order to ensure the survival of the next generation. Judah had learned from his own tragic experience that it was sometimes necessary to let go.

And so the brothers returned. When Joseph set eyes on Benjamin, the narrator tells us, "he was overcome with affection for his brother, and he was about to weep. So he went into a private room and wept there" (43:30). It is rare for the Bible to explain a character's inner feelings to us. The pain and rage that had hardened during Joseph's twenty-two years in Egypt were beginning to melt. But he was not yet so transformed that he had lost all his old desire to dominate. He engineered yet another test for the brothers, which ended with his threatening to keep Benjamin behind with him in Egypt— a loss that Jacob would be unable to sustain.

Finally, however, it was Judah, not Joseph, who brought about the reconciliation and final denouement. In an impassioned speech (44:18–32) he accepted full responsibility for the crimes of his family. Twenty-two years earlier, he had been ready to sell his brother into slavery. Now he was prepared to remain in Egypt as a slave to ensure that Benjamin went free. He had learned what it was like to lose beloved sons; he had learned to empathize with Jacob and to forgive him for the years of indifference and neglect. Judah had been able to accept the painful truth that had torn siblings apart since the time of Cain: that love is unfair. Only when we accept this and make peace with past pain and rejection can we move positively into the future as whole human beings. Instead of allowing his own tragedies to sour and fester, Judah had used them imaginatively to heal past wounds. His own suffering had enabled him to enter the inner world of the father who had wronged him. Judah had also learned from his experience with Tamar that it is only when we admit that we have been wrong that we can take full control of our lives and stop the ongoing cycle of violence, deception, and reprisal that holds us in thrall. Twenty-two years before, Judah had stood silently, watching Jacob weep over Joseph's robe. Now he could not endure the thought of his father going through that again for Benjamin. "Let your servant remain as a slave to my lord in place of the boy," he implored Joseph. "For how can I go back to my father if the boy is not with me? I fear to see the suffering that would come upon my father" (44:33–34). At last, one member of the family had learned compassion.

A Happy Ending?

JOSEPH WAS PROFOUNDLY MOVED BY JUDAH'S plea. Yet again he burst into tears and sobbed "so loudly that the Egyptians heard it, and the household of Pharaoh heard it" (45:2). "I am Joseph," he told his astonished brethren. "Is my father still alive?" (45:3). In this emotional extremity, he suddenly understood the meaning of his own extraordinary life. He could forgive his brothers, he told them, because they had only been God's tools. They had all thought that they were in charge of their own lives, but in reality they had simply been in God's hands. God had arranged for Joseph to be brought to Egypt to ensure that his chosen family would survive the famine. "And now do not be distressed, or angry with yourselves, because you sold me here," he told them, "for God sent me before you to preserve life . . . to preserve for you a remnant on earth, and to keep alive for you many survivors"

(45:5, 7). Had he not become vizier of Egypt, the whole family would have died of hunger in Canaan.

Yet for all the tears and drama, this was no sentimental Hollywood finale. The only person weeping, apart from Benjamin, was Joseph himself. He was the only one who spoke. What was going through the minds of the sons of Leah and the concubines as they watched Rachel's two children sobbing on each other's shoulders? Did they all share Judah's insight? Or were they—as seems only too likely—still trapped in the old hatred? We have seen the brothers standing silently, while others wept and pleaded, on other occasions. Was this silence any less implacable than their silent obduracy to Joseph's entreaties as they flung him into the pit? Joseph's speech has certain disquieting elements. As we watch him heaping coals of fire upon the guilty heads of his brothers, we realize that he was still full of the egotism that had helped to cause his suffering. *He* was the chosen deliverer; *he* would be the provider! His continual harping on his success and high rank is unpleasant in these circumstances:

> "And now your eyes and the eyes of my brother Benjamin see that it is my own mouth that speaks to you. You must tell my father how greatly I am honored in Egypt, and all that you have seen." (45:12–13)

We cannot help remembering his insensitive boasting in the past. But Joseph himself did not seem to recognize his own contribution to past tragedy. He had not confronted his own faults but, still possessed by dreams of grandeur, he set himself firmly at center stage. There is something insulting in the way he completely discounted his brethren's responsibility for their crime; to acknowledge that they had indeed been masters of their own destiny might have made him face the painful fact that they had some reason for their hatred and that he himself was not altogether blameless. Genesis as a whole does not accept this theological view of a wholly omnipotent and irresistible God, in whose grand design human beings are mere pawns. From a very early stage, the biblical authors suggested, God lost control of his creation. He had given humanity free will, and that meant that they shared his sovereign freedom. This alone should make us question Joseph's theology and his interpretation of events.

As Joseph walked around the family circle, weeping, talking compulsively, and embracing each brother in turn, the brethren stood dumbfounded. In a text in which dialogue has been so important, the brothers' silence and Joseph's utter lack of interest in their feelings must be significant. Like his father, Joseph had a streak of self-indulgence and egotism; he imagined that *his* emotions and experience alone were important and worthy of discussion. He had not achieved a total conversion and transformation. The authors leave us with the suggestion that, in fact, this reconciliation was no more complete than that of Jacob and Esau. The brothers did persuade the aged Jacob to settle in Egypt; the family was reunited. But when Jacob finally died, seventeen years later, the brothers were filled with fear. "What if Joseph still bears a grudge against us and pays us back in full for all the wrong that we did to him?" (50:15). All this time, they had worried about his intentions and had never fully trusted him. Joseph had to reassure them yet again, reminding them that even though *they* had thought they were responsible for the crime against him, they had really been God's instruments. The attentive reader of Genesis cannot accept this. And indeed, it has been clear throughout that for all Joseph's talk about God's omnipotence, he really believed that *he* was the one in control. He had played God in attempting to mastermind the repentance of his brothers and had learned nothing from the fact that it was Judah, not himself, who had made the reconciliation possible—not by discounting all responsibility for his sins but by acknowledging them fully.

Jacob's Blessing

 JOSEPH CLEARLY REGARDED THE LATTER PART of Genesis as "The Joseph Story." But the text makes it clear that in fact his story was simply part of the long saga of Jacob. The climax of Genesis is not the reconciliation scene of Chapter 45 but the elaborate blessing that Jacob gave to his sons, the ancestors of the twelve tribes of Israel. When we read that "the eyes of Israel were dim with age, and he could not see well" (48:10), we expect the worst. This is disturbingly reminiscent of Isaac's deathbed, and we have come to equate blindness with spiritual obtuseness. But at the last moment, the biblical writers confound our expectations. To our surprise, Jacob rose to the occasion and died a better man than he had lived. He adopted Joseph's two sons, Manasseh and Ephraim, giving Ephraim, the younger, precedence over Manasseh in deference to his God's habitual preference for younger siblings. When Joseph tried to correct him, he said gently, "I know, my son, I know" (48:19). He was informing Joseph not only that he was still in possession of his faculties but that he had knowledge of the ways of the perplexing deity he had encountered earlier in his life. Finally, Jacob gave instructions that he be buried not beside the beloved Rachel in Bethlehem but beside Leah in the family tomb at Hebron. For once, he did not allow himself to give in to his own inclinations but fulfilled his official patriarchal duty.

Before he died, Jacob achieved prophetic status, as he gave each of his sons a blessing and told them what was in store for their descendants. Each son had his own particular blessing and some were promised a better fate than others. Genesis reminds us once again that God—like life—is not fair. The point of blessing is not to give everybody the same but to enable each man to fulfill his potential. (Sadly, the Israelites did not bless their daughters.) Reuben lost his claim to leadership because of his earlier impious attempt to oust his father. Simeon and Levi were excluded from blessing; they were cursed because of their part in the massacre of Shechem. Instead, the leadership went to Judah, who had proved himself the wisest of the brothers. Joseph, nonetheless, remained Jacob's favorite: his blessing evoked all the richness, fertility, and harmony with creation that was the goal of early Israelite religion:

> Blessings of heaven above,
> blessings of the deep that lies beneath,
> blessings of the breasts and of the womb.
> The blessings of your father
> are stronger than the blessings of the eternal mountains,
> the bounties of the everlasting hills;
> may they be on the head of Joseph,
> on the brow of him who was set apart from his brothers.
> (49:25–27)

Yet Jacob's confidence in the potency of his blessing was misplaced. In the later history of Israel, as every reader of Genesis would know, Judah became the most important of the tribes and produced the royal house. The tribe of Joseph, however, fell into relative insignificance. Jacob was by no means omniscient. Some of his predictions were wrong: the tribe of Levi was not accursed and shunned. It produced Moses, the greatest Israelite of all, and the Levites would become the priestly tribe, the proud possessors of the unique privilege of serving Yahweh in the Temple. Right up to its last pages, the book of Genesis reminds us that there is no final certainty. Nobody is allowed to have the last word.

No Last Word

THROUGHOUT, THE AUTHORS OF GENESIS have been at pains to remind us that we can expect no clear-cut answers. From the very first sentence, we have had to wrestle with the text, and in the course of that struggle we may, like Jacob, have a brief moment of illumination. Genesis offers few consistent doctrines. Its teachings are frequently contradictory. What, for example, does it tell us about God? That he is omnipotent but powerless to control humanity; omniscient but ignorant of human yearning; creative but a destroyer; benevolent but a killer; wise but arbitrary; just but partial and unfair. Genesis points out that, as the most eminent monotheists have since emphasized, we cannot understand God or predict his behavior. The sacred reality must always remain an ineffable mystery which fills us with dread but exerts a ceaseless attraction. Our world is beautiful, baffling, and tragic. When we hear of devastating natural catastrophes or contemplate the millions of starving, suffering human beings, it is sometimes impossible, if we are honest, to imagine that the benevolent, omnipotent God of the first chapter of Genesis is really in control of his creation. Our day-to-day experience of the divine is more like the rest of Genesis, our insights fitful, transient, paradoxical, and ambiguous.

Survival is an important theme in Genesis. Banished from Eden, human beings had to struggle to remain physically, morally, and spiritually intact. Most of us get damaged at some point along the way. Genesis is true to life here. It shows us no paragons. Even the great patriarchs of Israel have feet of clay. Moments of grace and inspiration in their lives are frequently followed by episodes which show these men to be as flawed, negligent, self-indulgent, apathetic, and egotistical as any of us lesser mortals. Genesis does not provide us with people who have achieved virtue. Its stories are nothing like the lives of the saints that I was given to read as a child, which depicted these men and women as impossibly and depressingly flawless. The biblical authors do not seem to think that that kind of moral perfection is possible. Instead, they show us individuals struggling, like Jacob, for insight and the state which they call blessing.

From the first, Genesis teaches that a blessed life is possible for all creatures; we can all find our correct element and thrive therein. But Genesis also shows that it is more difficult for human beings than for other creatures to remain in the place allotted to them. We are conflicted and torn, tempted by the evil inclination, which is the source of some of our more brilliant cultural achievements as well as of our greatest crimes. Adam and Eve wanted knowledge. Like many religious people, they tried to attain privileged information. But the inescapable message of Genesis is that blessing and enlightenment are not achieved by acquiring facts and believing doctrines. Genesis gives us, as we have seen, no coherent theology but seems to frustrate our desire for clarity at every turn. Instead, knowledge means self-knowledge and an understanding of the mystery of our own being. We also have to recognize the sacred mystery of our fellow men and women. To seal ourselves off from others, like Noah in the Ark, can only lead to disintegration and abuse. The most memorable moments of blessing and revelation come from dynamic encounters with others, such as when Abraham rushed out to greet the strangers at Mamre and met his God, or when Jacob wrestled with God and found that he had been struggling with his brother and with his own self.

If Genesis does not allow us to make assumptions about God, it also refuses to let us imagine that we can fully comprehend one another. The patriarchs constantly surprise and even shock us; right up to the end, we are in the dark about the true feelings of Joseph and his brothers. Other human beings remain as opaque and mysterious as God—indeed, they can reveal to us the essential mystery and otherness of the sacred. Genesis traces God's gradual disappearance from the human scene. By the end, God no longer speaks or intervenes directly, and human beings can achieve the integration and wholeness for which they long only by coming to terms with their own natures, their own crimes, grief, and resentment. We have to make peace with the past, as best we can. It is a struggle in which we may never fully succeed, but only if it is undertaken can we become a source of blessing to the world and to others.

THE BOOK OF GENESIS

GENESIS

1 ¶1 In the beginning when God created the heavens and the earth, ¶2 the earth was a formless void and darkness covered the face of the deep, while a wind from God swept over the face of the waters. ¶3 Then God said, "Let there be light"; and there was light. ¶4 And God saw that the light was good; and God separated the light from the darkness. ¶5 God called the light Day, and the darkness he called Night. And there was evening and there was morning, the first day. ¶6 And God said, "Let there be a dome in the midst of the waters, and let it separate the waters from the waters." ¶7 So God made the dome and separated the waters that were under the dome from the waters that were above the dome. And it was so. ¶8 God called the dome Sky. And there was evening and there was morning, the second day. ¶9 And God said, "Let the waters under the sky be gathered together into one place, and let the dry land appear." And it was so. ¶10 God called the dry land Earth, and the waters that were gathered together he called Seas. And God saw that it was good. ¶11 Then God said, "Let the earth put forth vegetation: plants yielding seed, and fruit trees of every kind on earth that bear fruit with the seed in it." And it was so. ¶12 The earth brought forth vegetation: plants yielding seed of every kind, and trees of every kind bearing fruit with the seed in it. And God saw that it was good. ¶13 And there was evening and there was morning, the third day. ¶14 And God said, "Let there be lights in the dome of the sky to separate the day from the night; and let them be for signs and for seasons and for days and years, ¶15 and let them be lights in the dome of the sky to give light upon the earth." And it was so. ¶16 God made the two great lights—the greater light to rule the day and the lesser light to rule the night—and the stars. ¶17 God set them in the dome of the sky to give light upon the earth, ¶18 to rule over the day and over the night, and to separate the light from the darkness. And God saw that it was good. ¶19 And there was evening and there was morning, the fourth day. ¶20 And God said, "Let the waters bring forth swarms of living creatures, and let birds fly above the earth across the dome of the sky." ¶21 So God created the great sea monsters and every living creature that moves, of every kind, with which the waters swarm, and every winged bird of every kind. And God saw that it was good. ¶22 God blessed them, saying, "Be fruitful and multiply and fill the waters in the seas,

and let birds multiply on the earth." ¶23 And there was evening and there was morning, the fifth day. ¶24 And God said, "Let the earth bring forth living creatures of every kind: cattle and creeping things and wild animals of the earth of every kind." And it was so. ¶25 God made the wild animals of the earth of every kind, and the cattle of every kind, and everything that creeps upon the ground of every kind. And God saw that it was good. ¶26 Then God said, "Let us make humankind in our image, according to our likeness; and let them have dominion over the fish of the sea, and over the birds of the air, and over the cattle, and over all the wild animals of the earth, and over every creeping thing that creeps upon the earth." ¶27 *So God created humankind in his image, in the image of God he created them; male and female he created them.* ¶28 God blessed them, and God said to them, "Be fruitful and multiply, and fill the earth and subdue it; and have dominion over the fish of the sea and over the birds of the air and over every living thing that moves upon the earth." ¶29 God said, "See, I have given you every plant yielding seed that is upon the face of all the earth, and every tree with seed in its fruit; you shall have them for food. ¶30 And to every beast of the earth, and to every bird of the air, and to everything that creeps on the earth, everything that has the breath of life, I have given every green plant for food." And it was so. ¶31 God saw everything that he had made, and indeed, it was very good. And there was evening and there was morning, the sixth day.

2 ¶1 Thus the heavens and the earth were finished, and all their multitude. ¶2 And on the seventh day God finished the work that he had done, and he rested on the seventh day from all the work that he had done. ¶3 So God blessed the seventh day and hallowed it, because on it God rested from all the work that he had done in creation. ¶4 These are the generations of the heavens and the earth when they were created. In the day that the LORD God made the earth and the heavens, ¶5 when no plant of the field was yet in the earth and no herb of the field had yet sprung up—for the LORD God had not caused it to rain upon the earth, and there was no one to till the ground; ¶6 but a stream would rise from the earth, and water the whole face of the ground— ¶7 then the LORD God formed man from the dust of the ground, and breathed into his nostrils the breath of life; and the man became a living being. ¶8 And the LORD God planted a garden in Eden, in the east; and there he put the man whom he had formed. ¶9 Out of the ground the LORD God made to grow every tree that is pleasant to the sight and good for food, the tree of life also in the midst of the garden, and the tree of the knowledge of good and evil. ¶10 A river flows out of Eden to water the garden, and from there it divides and becomes four branches. ¶11 The name of the first is Pishon; it is the one that flows around the whole land of Havilah, where there is gold; ¶12 and the gold of that land is good; bdellium and onyx stone are there. ¶13 The name of the second river is Gihon; it is the one that flows around the whole land of Cush. ¶14 The name of the third river is Tigris, which flows east of

Assyria. And the fourth river is the Euphrates. ¶15 The LORD God took the man and put him in the garden of Eden to till it and keep it. ¶16 And the LORD God commanded the man, "You may freely eat of every tree of the garden; ¶17 but of the tree of the knowledge of good and evil you shall not eat, for in the day that you eat of it you shall die." ¶18 Then the LORD God said, "It is not good that the man should be alone; I will make him a helper as his partner." ¶19 So out of the ground the LORD God formed every animal of the field and every bird of the air, and brought them to the man to see what he would call them; and whatever the man called every living creature, that was its name. ¶20 The man gave names to all cattle, and to the birds of the air, and to every animal of the field; but for the man there was not found a helper as his partner. ¶21 So the LORD God caused a deep sleep to fall upon the man, and he slept; then he took one of his ribs and closed up its place with flesh. ¶22 And the rib that the LORD God had taken from the man he made into a woman and brought her to the man. ¶23 Then the man said, *"This at last is bone of my bones and flesh of my flesh; this one shall be called Woman, for out of Man this one was taken."* ¶24 Therefore a man leaves his father and his mother and clings to his wife, and they become one flesh. ¶25 And the man and his wife were both naked, and were not ashamed.

3 ¶1 Now the serpent was more crafty than any other wild animal that the LORD God had made. He said to the woman, "Did God say, 'You shall not eat

from any tree in the garden'?" ¶2 The woman said to the serpent, "We may eat of the fruit of the trees in the garden; ¶3 but God said, 'You shall not eat of the fruit of the tree that is in the middle of the garden, nor shall you touch it, or you shall die.' " ¶4 But the serpent said to the woman, "You will not die; ¶5 for God knows that when you eat of it your eyes will be opened, and you will be like God, knowing good and evil." ¶6 So when the woman saw that the tree was good for food, and that it was a delight to the eyes, and that the tree was to be desired to make one wise, she took of its fruit and ate; and she also gave some to her husband, who was with her, and he ate. ¶7 Then the eyes of both were opened, and they knew that they were naked; and they sewed fig leaves together and made loincloths for themselves. ¶8 They heard the sound of the LORD God walking in the garden at the time of the evening breeze, and the man and his wife hid themselves from the presence of the LORD God among the trees of the garden. ¶9 But the LORD God called to the man, and said to him, "Where are you?" ¶10 He said, "I heard the sound of you in the garden, and I was afraid, because I was naked; and I hid myself." ¶11 He said, "Who told you that you were naked? Have you eaten from the tree of which I commanded you not to eat?" ¶12 The man said, "The woman whom you gave to be with me, she gave me fruit from the tree, and I ate." ¶13 Then the LORD God said to the woman, "What is this that you have done?" The woman said, "The serpent tricked me, and I ate." ¶14 The LORD God said to the serpent, *"Because you have done this, cursed are you among all animals and among all wild creatures; upon your belly you shall go, and dust you shall eat all the days of your life.* ¶15 *I will put enmity between you and the woman, and between your offspring and hers; he will strike your head, and you will strike his heel."* ¶16 To the woman he said, *"I will greatly increase your pangs in childbearing; in pain you shall bring forth children, yet your desire shall be for your husband, and he shall rule over you."* ¶17 And to the man he said, *"Because you have listened to the voice of your wife, and have eaten of the tree about which I commanded you, 'You shall not eat of it,' cursed is the ground because of you; in toil you shall eat of it all the days of your life;* ¶18 *thorns and thistles it shall bring forth for you; and you shall eat the plants of the field.* ¶19 *By the sweat of your face you shall eat bread until you return to the ground, for out of it you were taken; you are dust, and to dust you shall return."* ¶20 The man named his wife Eve, because she was the mother of all living. ¶21 And the LORD God made garments of skins for the man and for his wife, and clothed them. ¶22 Then the LORD God said, "See, the man has become like one of us, knowing good and evil; and now, he might reach out his hand and take also from the tree of life, and eat, and live forever"— ¶23 therefore the LORD God sent him forth from the garden of Eden, to till the ground from which he was taken. ¶24 He drove out the man; and at the east of the garden of Eden he placed the cherubim, and a sword flaming and turning to guard the way to the tree of life.

4 ¶1 Now the man knew his wife Eve, and she conceived and bore Cain, saying, "I have produced a man with the help of the LORD." ¶2 Next she bore his brother Abel. Now Abel was a keeper of sheep, and Cain a tiller of the ground. ¶3 In the course of time Cain brought to the LORD an offering of the fruit of the ground, ¶4 and Abel for his part brought of the firstlings of his flock, their fat portions. And the LORD had regard for Abel and his offering, ¶5 but for Cain and his offering he had no regard. So Cain was very angry, and his countenance fell. ¶6 The LORD said to Cain, "Why are you angry, and why has your countenance fallen? ¶7 If you do well, will you not be accepted? And if you do not do well, sin is lurking at the door; its desire is for you, but you must master it." ¶8 Cain said to his brother Abel, "Let us go out to the field." And when they were in the field, Cain rose up against his brother Abel, and killed him. ¶9 Then the LORD said to Cain, "Where is your brother Abel?" He said, "I do not know; am I my brother's keeper?" ¶10 And the LORD said, "What have you done? Listen; your brother's blood is crying out to me from the ground! ¶11 And now you are cursed from the ground, which has opened its mouth to receive your brother's blood from your hand. ¶12 When you till the ground, it will no longer yield to you its strength; you will be a fugitive and a wanderer on the earth." ¶13 Cain said to the LORD, "My punishment is greater than I can bear! ¶14 Today you have driven me away from the soil, and I shall be hidden from your face; I shall be a fugitive and a wanderer on the earth, and anyone who meets me may kill me." ¶15 Then the LORD said to him, "Not so! Whoever kills Cain will suffer a sevenfold vengeance." And the LORD put a mark on Cain, so that no one who came upon him would kill him. ¶16 Then Cain went

away from the presence of the LORD, and settled in the land of Nod, east of Eden. ¶17 Cain knew his wife, and she conceived and bore Enoch; and he built a city, and named it Enoch after his son Enoch. ¶18 To Enoch was born Irad; and Irad was the father of Mehujael, and Mehujael the father of Methushael, and Methushael the father of Lamech. ¶19 Lamech took two wives; the name of the one was Adah, and the name of the other Zillah. ¶20 Adah bore Jabal; he was the ancestor of those who live in tents and have livestock. ¶21 His brother's name was Jubal; he was the ancestor of all those who play the lyre and pipe. ¶22 Zillah bore Tubal-cain, who made all kinds of bronze and iron tools. The sister of Tubal-cain was Naamah. ¶23 Lamech said to his wives: *"Adah and Zillah, hear my voice; you wives of Lamech, listen to what I say: I have killed a man for wounding me, a young man for striking me. ¶24 If Cain is avenged sevenfold, truly Lamech seventy-sevenfold."* ¶25 Adam knew his wife again, and she bore a son and named him Seth, for she said, "God has appointed for me another child instead of Abel, because Cain killed him." ¶26 To Seth also a son was born, and he named him Enosh. At that time people began to invoke the name of the LORD.

5 ¶1 This is the list of the descendants of Adam. When God created humankind, he made them in the likeness of God. ¶2 Male and female he created them, and he blessed them and named them "Humankind" when they were created. ¶3 When Adam had lived one hundred thirty years, he became the father of a son in his likeness, according to his image, and named him Seth. ¶4 The days of Adam after he became the father of Seth were eight hundred years; and he had other sons and daughters. ¶5 Thus all the days that Adam lived were nine hundred thirty years, and he died. ¶6 When Seth had lived one hundred five years, he became the father of Enosh. ¶7 Seth lived after the birth of Enosh eight hundred seven years, and had other sons and daughters. ¶8 Thus all the days of Seth were nine hundred twelve years; and he died. ¶9 When Enosh had lived ninety years, he became the father of Kenan. ¶10 Enosh lived after the birth of Kenan eight hundred fifteen years, and had other sons and daughters. ¶11 Thus all the days of Enosh were nine hundred five years; and he died. ¶12 When Kenan had lived seventy years, he became the father of Mahalalel. ¶13 Kenan lived after the birth of Mahalalel eight hundred and forty years, and had other sons and daughters. ¶14 Thus all the days of Kenan were nine hundred and ten years; and he died. ¶15 When Mahalalel had lived sixty-five years, he became the father of Jared. ¶16 Mahalalel lived after the birth of Jared eight hundred thirty years, and had other sons and daughters. ¶17 Thus all the days of Mahalalel were eight hundred ninety-five years; and he died. ¶18 When Jared had lived one hundred sixty-two years he became the father of Enoch. ¶19 Jared lived after the birth of Enoch eight hundred years, and had other sons and daughters. ¶20 Thus all the days of Jared were nine hundred sixty-two years; and he died. ¶21 When Enoch had lived sixty-five years, he became the father of Methuselah. ¶22 Enoch walked

with God after the birth of Methuselah three hundred years, and had other sons and daughters. ¶23 Thus all the days of Enoch were three hundred sixty-five years. ¶24 Enoch walked with God; then he was no more, because God took him. ¶25 When Methuselah had lived one hundred eighty-seven years, he became the father of Lamech. ¶26 Methuselah lived after the birth of Lamech seven hundred eighty-two years, and had other sons and daughters. ¶27 Thus all the days of Methuselah were nine hundred sixty-nine years; and he died. ¶28 When Lamech had lived one hundred eighty-two years, he became the father of a son; ¶29 he named him Noah, saying, "Out of the ground that the LORD has cursed this one shall bring us relief from our work and from the toil of our hands." ¶30 Lamech lived after the birth of Noah five hundred ninety-five years, and had other sons and daughters. ¶31 Thus all the days of Lamech were seven hundred seventy-seven years; and he died. ¶32 After Noah was five hundred years old, Noah became the father of Shem, Ham, and Japheth.

6 ¶1 When people began to multiply on the face of the ground, and daughters were born to them, ¶2 the sons of God saw that they were fair; and they took wives for themselves of all that they chose. ¶3 Then the LORD said, "My spirit shall not abide in mortals forever, for they are flesh; their days shall be one hundred twenty years." ¶4 The Nephilim were on the earth in those days—and also afterward—when the sons of God went in to the daughters of humans, who bore children to them. These were the heroes that were of old, warriors of renown. ¶5 The LORD saw that the wickedness of humankind was great in the earth, and that every inclination of the thoughts of their hearts was only evil continually. ¶6 And the LORD was sorry that he had made humankind on the earth, and it grieved him to his heart. ¶7 So the LORD said, "I will blot out from the earth the human beings I have created—people together with animals and creeping things and birds of the air, for I am sorry that I have made them." ¶8 But Noah found favor in the sight of the LORD. ¶9 These are the descendants of Noah. Noah was a righteous man, blameless in his generation; Noah walked with God. ¶10 And Noah had three sons, Shem, Ham, and Japheth. ¶11 Now the earth was corrupt in God's sight, and the earth was filled with violence. ¶12 And God saw that the earth was corrupt; for all flesh had corrupted its ways upon the earth. ¶13 And God said to Noah, "I have determined to make an end of all flesh, for the earth is filled with violence because of them; now I am going to destroy them along with the earth. ¶14 Make yourself an ark of cypress wood; make rooms in the ark, and cover it inside and out with pitch. ¶15 This is how you are to make it: the length of the ark three hundred cubits, its width fifty cubits, and its height thirty cubits. ¶16 Make a roof for the ark, and finish it to a cubit above; and put the door of the ark in its side; make it with lower, second, and third decks. ¶17 For my part, I am going to bring a flood of waters on the earth, to destroy from under heaven all flesh in which is the breath of

life; everything that is on the earth shall die. ¶18 But I will establish my covenant with you; and you shall come into the ark, you, your sons, your wife, and your sons' wives with you. ¶19 And of every living thing, of all flesh, you shall bring two of every kind into the ark, to keep them alive with you; they shall be male and female. ¶20 Of the birds according to their kinds, and of the animals according to their kinds, of every creeping thing of the ground according to its kind, two of every kind shall come in to you, to keep them alive. ¶21 Also take with you every kind of food that is eaten, and store it up; and it shall serve as food for you and for them." ¶22 Noah did this; he did all that God commanded him.

¶1 Then the LORD said to Noah, "Go into the ark, you and all your household, for I have seen that you alone are righteous before me in this generation. ¶2 Take with you seven pairs of all clean animals, the male and its mate; and a pair of the animals that are not clean, the male and its mate; ¶3 and seven pairs of the birds of the air also, male and female, to keep their kind alive on the face of all the earth. ¶4 For in seven days I will send rain on the earth for forty days and forty nights; and every living thing that I have made I will blot out from the face of the ground." ¶5 And Noah did all that the LORD had commanded him. ¶6 Noah was six hundred years old when the flood of waters came on the earth. ¶7 And Noah with his sons and his wife and his sons' wives went into the ark to escape the waters of the flood. ¶8 Of clean animals, and of animals that are not clean, and of birds, and of everything that creeps on the ground, ¶9 two and two, male and female, went into the ark with Noah, as God had commanded Noah. ¶10 And after seven days the waters of the flood came on the earth. ¶11 In the six hundredth year of Noah's life, in the second month, on the seventeenth day of the month, on that day all the fountains of the great deep burst forth, and the windows of the heavens were opened. ¶12 The rain fell on the earth forty days and forty nights. ¶13 On the very same day Noah with his sons, Shem and Ham and Japheth, and Noah's wife and the three wives of his sons entered the ark, ¶14 they and every wild animal of every kind, and all domestic animals of every kind, and every creeping thing that creeps on the earth, and every bird of every kind—every bird, every winged creature. ¶15 They went into the ark with Noah, two and two of all flesh in which there was the breath of life. ¶16 And those that entered, male and female of all flesh, went in as God had commanded him; and the LORD shut him in. ¶17 The flood continued forty days on the earth; and the waters increased, and bore up the ark, and it rose high above the earth. ¶18 The waters swelled and increased greatly on the earth; and the ark floated on the face of the waters. ¶19 The waters swelled so mightily on the earth that all the high mountains under the whole heaven were covered; ¶20 the waters swelled above the mountains, covering them fifteen cubits deep. ¶21 And all flesh died that moved on the earth, birds, domestic animals, wild animals, all swarming creatures that swarm on the earth, and all human beings; ¶22 everything on dry land in whose nostrils was the breath of life died. ¶23 He blotted out every living thing that was on the face of the ground, human beings and animals and creeping things and birds of the air; they were blotted out from the earth. Only Noah was left, and those that were with him in the ark. ¶24 And the waters swelled on the earth for one hundred fifty days.

8 ¶1 But God remembered Noah and all the wild animals and all the domestic animals that were with him in the ark. And God made a wind blow over the earth, and the waters subsided; ¶2 the fountains of the deep and the windows of the heavens were closed, the rain from the heavens was restrained, ¶3 and the waters gradually receded from the earth. At the end of one hundred fifty days the waters had abated; ¶4 and in the seventh month, on the seventeenth day of the month, the ark came to rest on the mountains of Ararat. ¶5 The waters continued to abate until the tenth month; in the tenth month, on the first day of the month, the tops of the mountains appeared. ¶6 At the end of forty days Noah opened the window of the ark that he had made ¶7 and sent out the raven; and it went to and fro until the waters were dried up from the earth. ¶8 Then he sent out the dove from him, to see if the waters had subsided from the face of the ground; ¶9 but the dove found no place to set its foot, and it returned to him to the ark, for the waters were still on the face of the whole earth. So he put out his hand and took it and brought it into the ark with him. ¶10 He waited another seven days, and again he sent out the dove from the ark; ¶11 and the dove came back to him in the evening, and there in its beak was a freshly plucked olive leaf; so Noah knew that the waters had subsided from the earth. ¶12 Then he waited another seven days, and sent out the dove; and it did not return to him any more. ¶13 In the six hundred first year, in the first month, the first day of the month, the waters were dried up from the earth; and Noah removed the covering of the ark, and looked, and saw that the face of the ground was drying. ¶14 In the second month, on the twenty-seventh day of the month, the earth was dry. ¶15 Then God said to Noah, ¶16 "Go out of the ark, you and your wife, and your sons and your sons' wives with you. ¶17 Bring out with you every living thing that is with you of all flesh—birds and animals and every creeping thing that creeps on the earth—so that they may abound on the earth, and be fruitful and multiply on the earth." ¶18 So Noah went out with his sons and his wife and his sons' wives. ¶19 And every animal, every creeping thing, and every bird, everything that moves on the earth, went out of the ark by families. ¶20 Then Noah built an altar to the LORD, and took of every clean animal and of every clean bird, and offered burnt offerings on the altar. ¶21 And when the LORD smelled the pleasing odor, the LORD said in his heart, "I will never again curse the ground because of humankind, for the inclination of the human heart is evil from youth; nor will I ever again destroy every living creature as I have done. ¶22 *As long as the earth en-*

dures, seedtime and harvest, cold and heat, summer and winter, day and night, shall not cease."

9 ¶1 God blessed Noah and his sons, and said to them, "Be fruitful and multiply, and fill the earth. ¶2 The fear and dread of you shall rest on every animal of the earth, and on every bird of the air, on everything that creeps on the ground, and on all the fish of the sea; into your hand they are delivered. ¶3 Every moving thing that lives shall be food for you; and just as I gave you the green plants, I give you everything. ¶4 Only, you shall not eat flesh with its life, that is, its blood. ¶5 For your own lifeblood I will surely require a reckoning: from every animal I will require it and from human beings, each one for the blood of another, I will require a reckoning for human life.
¶6 *Whoever sheds the blood of a human, by a human shall that person's blood be shed; for in his own image God made humankind.* ¶7 And you, be fruitful and multiply, abound on the earth and multiply in it." ¶8 Then God said to Noah and to his sons with him, ¶9 "As for me, I am establishing my covenant with you and your descendants after you, ¶10 and with every living creature that is with you, the birds, the domestic animals, and every animal of the earth with you, as many as came out of the ark. ¶11 I establish my covenant with you, that never again shall all flesh be cut off by the waters of a flood, and never again shall there be a flood to destroy the earth." ¶12 God said, "This is the sign of the covenant that I make between me and you

and every living creature that is with you, for all future generations: ¶13 I have set my bow in the clouds, and it shall be a sign of the covenant between me and the earth. ¶14 When I bring clouds over the earth and the bow is seen in the clouds, ¶15 I will remember my covenant that is between me and you and every living creature of all flesh; and the waters shall never again become a flood to destroy all flesh. ¶16 When the bow is in the clouds, I will see it and remember the everlasting covenant between God and every living creature of all flesh that is on the earth." ¶17 God said to Noah, "This is the sign of the covenant that I have established between me and all flesh that is on the earth." ¶18 The sons of Noah who went out of the ark were Shem, Ham, and Japheth. Ham was the father of Canaan. ¶19 These three were the sons of Noah; and from these the whole earth was peopled. ¶20 Noah, a man of the soil, was the first to plant a vineyard. ¶21 He drank some of the wine and became drunk, and he lay uncovered in his tent. ¶22 And Ham, the father of Canaan, saw the nakedness of his father, and told his two brothers outside. ¶23 Then Shem and Japheth took a garment, laid it on both their shoulders, and walked backward and covered the nakedness of their father; their faces were turned away, and they did not see their father's nakedness. ¶24 When Noah awoke from his wine and knew what his youngest son had done to him, ¶25 he said, *"Cursed be Canaan; lowest of slaves shall he be to his brothers."* ¶26 He also said, *"Blessed by the* LORD *my God be Shem; and let Canaan be his slave.*

¶27 *May God make space for Japheth, and let him live in the tents of Shem; and let Canaan be his slave."* ¶28 After the flood Noah lived three hundred fifty years. ¶29 All the days of Noah were nine hundred fifty years; and he died.

10 ¶1 These are the descendants of Noah's sons, Shem, Ham, and Japheth; children were born to them after the flood. ¶2 The descendants of Japheth: Gomer, Magog, Madai, Javan, Tubal, Meshech, and Tiras. ¶3 The descendants of Gomer: Ashkenaz, Riphath, and Togarmah. ¶4 The descendants of Javan: Elishah, Tarshish, Kittim, and Rodanim. ¶5 From these the coastland peoples spread. These are the descendants of Japheth in their lands, with their own language, by their families, in their nations. ¶6 The descendants of Ham: Cush, Egypt, Put, and Canaan. ¶7 The descendants of Cush: Seba, Havilah, Sabtah, Raamah, and Sabteca. The descendants of Raamah: Sheba and Dedan. ¶8 Cush became the father of Nimrod; he was the first on earth to become a mighty warrior. ¶9 He was a mighty hunter before the LORD; therefore it is said, "Like Nimrod a mighty hunter before the LORD." ¶10 The beginning of his kingdom was Babel, Erech, and Accad, all of them in the land of Shinar. ¶11 From that land he went into Assyria, and built Nineveh, Rehoboth-ir, Calah, and ¶12 Resen between Nineveh and Calah; that is the great city. ¶13 Egypt became the father of Ludim, Anamim, Lehabim, Naphtuhim, ¶14 Pathrusim, Casluhim, and Caphtorim, from which the

Philistines come. ¶15 Canaan became the father of Sidon his firstborn, and Heth, ¶16 and the Jebusites, the Amorites, the Girgashites, ¶17 the Hivites, the Arkites, the Sinites, ¶18 the Arvadites, the Zemarites, and the Hamathites. Afterward the families of the Canaanites spread abroad. ¶19 And the territory of the Canaanites extended from Sidon, in the direction of Gerar, as far as Gaza, and in the direction of Sodom, Gomorrah, Admah, and Zeboiim, as far as Lasha. ¶20 These are the descendants of Ham, by their families, their languages, their lands, and their nations. ¶21 To Shem also, the father of all the children of Eber, the elder brother of Japheth, children were born. ¶22 The descendants of Shem: Elam, Asshur, Arpachshad, Lud, and Aram. ¶23 The descendants of Aram: Uz, Hul, Gether, and Mash. ¶24 Arpachshad became the father of Shelah; and Shelah became the father of Eber. ¶25 To Eber were born two sons: the name of the one was Peleg, for in his days the earth was divided, and his brother's name was Joktan. ¶26 Joktan became the father of Almodad, Sheleph, Hazarmaveth, Jerah, ¶27 Hadoram, Uzal, Diklah, ¶28 Obal, Abimael, Sheba, ¶29 Ophir, Havilah, and Jobab; all these were the descendants of Joktan. ¶30 The territory in which they lived extended from Mesha in the direction of Sephar, the hill country of the east. ¶31 These are the descendants of Shem, by their families, their languages, their lands, and their nations. ¶32 These are the families of Noah's sons, according to their genealogies, in their nations; and from these the nations spread abroad on the earth after the flood.

11 ¶1 Now the whole earth had one language and the same words. ¶2 And as they migrated from the east, they came upon a plain in the land of Shinar and settled there. ¶3 And they said to one another, "Come, let us make bricks, and burn them thoroughly." And they had brick for stone, and bitumen for mortar. ¶4 Then they said, "Come, let us build ourselves a city, and a tower with its top in the heavens, and let us make a name for ourselves; otherwise we shall be scattered abroad upon the face of the whole earth." ¶5 The LORD came down to see the city and the tower, which mortals had built. ¶6 And the LORD said, "Look, they are one people, and they have all one language; and this is only the beginning of what they will do; nothing that they propose to do will now be impossible for them. ¶7 Come, let us go down, and confuse their language there, so that they will not understand one another's speech." ¶8 So the LORD scattered them abroad from there over the face of all the earth, and they left off building the city. ¶9 Therefore it was called Babel, because there the LORD confused the language of all the earth; and from there the LORD scattered them abroad over the face of all the earth. ¶10 These are the descendants of Shem. When Shem was one hundred years old, he became the father of Arpachshad two years after the flood; ¶11 and Shem lived after the birth of Arpachshad five hundred years, and had other sons and daughters. ¶12 When Arpachshad had lived thirty-five years, he became the father of Shelah; ¶13 and Arpachshad lived after the birth of Shelah four hundred three years, and had other sons and daughters. ¶14 When Shelah had lived thirty years, he became the father of Eber; ¶15 and Shelah lived after the birth of Eber four hundred three years, and had other sons and daughters. ¶16 When Eber had lived thirty-four years, he became the father of Peleg; ¶17 and Eber lived after the birth of Peleg four hundred thirty years, and had other sons and daughters. ¶18 When Peleg had lived thirty years, he became the father of Reu; ¶19 and Peleg lived after the birth of Reu two hundred nine years, and had other sons and daughters. ¶20 When Reu had lived thirty-two years, he became the father of Serug; ¶21 and Reu lived after the birth of Serug two hundred seven years, and had other sons and daughters. ¶22 When Serug had lived thirty years, he became the father of Nahor; ¶23 and Serug lived after the birth of Nahor two hundred years, and had other sons and daughters. ¶24 When Nahor had lived twenty-nine years, he became the father of Terah; ¶25 and Nahor lived after the birth of Terah one hundred nineteen years, and had other sons and daughters. ¶26 When Terah had lived seventy years, he became the father of Abram, Nahor, and Haran. ¶27 Now these are the descendants of Terah. Terah was the father of Abram, Nahor, and Haran; and Haran was the father of Lot. ¶28 Haran died before his father Terah in the land of his birth, in Ur of the Chaldeans. ¶29 Abram and Nahor took wives; the name of Abram's wife was Sarai, and the name of Nahor's wife was Milcah. She was the daughter of Haran the father of Milcah and Iscah. ¶30 Now Sarai was barren; she had no child. ¶31 Terah took his son Abram and his

grandson Lot son of Haran, and his daughter-in-law Sarai, his son Abram's wife, and they went out together from Ur of the Chaldeans to go into the land of Canaan; but when they came to Haran, they settled there. ¶32 The days of Terah were two hundred five years; and Terah died in Haran.

12 ¶1 Now the LORD said to Abram, "Go from your country and your kindred and your father's house to the land that I will show you. ¶2 I will make of you a great nation, and I will bless you, and make your name great, so that you will be a blessing. ¶3 I will bless those who bless you, and the one who curses you I will curse; and in you all the families of the earth shall be blessed." ¶4 So Abram went, as the LORD had told him; and Lot went with him. Abram was seventy-five years old when he departed from Haran. ¶5 Abram took his wife Sarai and his brother's son Lot, and all the possessions that they had gathered, and the persons whom they had acquired in Haran; and they set forth to go to the land of Canaan. When they had come to the land of Canaan, ¶6 Abram passed through the land to the place at Shechem, to the oak of Moreh. At that time the Canaanites were in the land. ¶7 Then the LORD appeared to Abram, and said, "To your offspring I will give this land." So he built there an altar to the LORD, who had appeared to him. ¶8 From there he moved on to the hill country on the east of Bethel, and pitched his tent, with Bethel on the west and Ai on the east; and there he built an altar to the LORD and invoked the name of the

LORD. ¶9 And Abram journeyed on by stages toward the Negeb. ¶10 Now there was a famine in the land. So Abram went down to Egypt to reside there as an alien, for the famine was severe in the land. ¶11 When he was about to enter Egypt, he said to his wife Sarai, "I know well that you are a woman beautiful in appearance; ¶12 and when the Egyptians see you, they will say, 'This is his wife'; then they will kill me, but they will let you live. ¶13 Say you are my sister, so that it may go well with me because of you, and that my life may be spared on your account." ¶14 When Abram entered Egypt the Egyptians saw that the woman was very beautiful. ¶15 When the officials of Pharaoh saw her, they praised her to Pharaoh. And the woman was taken into Pharaoh's house. ¶16 And for her sake he dealt well with Abram; and he had sheep, oxen, male donkeys, male and female slaves, female donkeys, and camels. ¶17 But the LORD afflicted Pharaoh and his house with great plagues because of Sarai, Abram's wife. ¶18 So Pharaoh called Abram, and said, "What is this you have done to me? Why did you not tell me that she was your wife? ¶19 Why did you say, 'She is my sister,' so that I took her for my wife? Now then, here is your wife, take her, and be gone." ¶20 And Pharaoh gave his men orders concerning him; and they set him on the way, with his wife and all that he had.

13 ¶1 So Abram went up from Egypt, he and his wife, and all that he had, and Lot with him, into the Negeb. ¶2 Now Abram was very

rich in livestock, in silver, and in gold. ¶3 He journeyed on by stages from the Negeb as far as Bethel, to the place where his tent had been at the beginning, between Bethel and Ai, ¶4 to the place where he had made an altar at the first; and there Abram called on the name of the LORD. ¶5 Now Lot, who went with Abram, also had flocks and herds and tents, ¶6 so that the land could not support both of them living together; for their possessions were so great that they could not live together, ¶7 and there was strife between the herders of Abram's livestock and the herders of Lot's livestock. At that time the Canaanites and the Perizzites lived in the land. ¶8 Then Abram said to Lot, "Let there be no strife between you and me, and between your herders and my herders; for we are kindred. ¶9 Is not the whole land before you? Separate yourself from me. If you take the left hand, then I will go to the right; or if you take the right hand, then I will go to the left." ¶10 Lot looked about him, and saw that the plain of the Jordan was well watered everywhere like the garden of the LORD, like the land of Egypt, in the direction of Zoar; this was before the LORD had destroyed Sodom and Gomorrah. ¶11 So Lot chose for himself all the plain of the Jordan, and Lot journeyed eastward; thus they separated from each other. ¶12 Abram settled in the land of Canaan, while Lot settled among the cities of the Plain and moved his tent as far as Sodom. ¶13 Now the people of Sodom were wicked, great sinners against the LORD. ¶14 The LORD said to Abram, after Lot had separated from him, "Raise your eyes now, and look from the place where you are, north-ward and southward and eastward and westward; ¶15 for all the land that you see I will give to you and to your offspring forever. ¶16 I will make your offspring like the dust of the earth; so that if one can count the dust of the earth, your offspring also can be counted. ¶17 Rise up, walk through the length and the breadth of the land, for I will give it to you." ¶18 So Abram moved his tent, and came and settled by the oaks of Mamre, which are at Hebron; and there he built an altar to the LORD.

14 ¶1 In the days of King Amraphel of Shinar, King Arioch of Ellasar, King Chedorlaomer of Elam, and King Tidal of Goiim, ¶2 these kings made war with King Bera of Sodom, King Birsha of Gomorrah, King Shinab of Admah, King Shemeber of Zeboiim, and the king of Bela (that is, Zoar). ¶3 All these joined forces in the Valley of Siddim (that is, the Dead Sea). ¶4 Twelve years they had served Chedorlaomer, but in the thirteenth year they rebelled. ¶5 In the fourteenth year Chedorlaomer and the kings who were with him came and subdued the Rephaim in Ashterothkarnaim, the Zuzim in Ham, the Emim in Shaveh-kiriathaim, ¶6 and the Horites in the hill country of Seir as far as Elparan on the edge of the wilderness; ¶7 then they turned back and came to Enmishpat (that is, Kadesh), and subdued all the country of the Amalekites, and also the Amorites who lived in Hazazon-tamar. ¶8 Then the king of Sodom, the king of Gomorrah, the king of Admah, the king of Zeboiim, and

the king of Bela (that is, Zoar) went out, and they joined battle in the Valley of Siddim ¶9 with King Chedorlaomer of Elam, King Tidal of Goiim, King Amraphel of Shinar, and King Arioch of Ellasar, four kings against five. ¶10 Now the Valley of Siddim was full of bitumen pits; and as the kings of Sodom and Gomorrah fled, some fell into them, and the rest fled to the hill country. ¶11 So the enemy took all the goods of Sodom and Gomorrah, and all their provisions, and went their way; ¶12 they also took Lot, the son of Abram's brother, who lived in Sodom, and his goods, and departed. ¶13 Then one who had escaped came and told Abram the Hebrew, who was living by the oaks of Mamre the Amorite, brother of Eshcol and of Aner; these were allies of Abram. ¶14 When Abram heard that his nephew had been taken captive, he led forth his trained men, born in his house, three hundred eighteen of them, and went in pursuit as far as Dan. ¶15 He divided his forces against them by night, he and his servants, and routed them and pursued them to Hobah, north of Damascus. ¶16 Then he brought back all the goods, and also brought back his nephew Lot with his goods, and the women and the people. ¶17 After his return from the defeat of Chedorlaomer and the kings who were with him, the king of Sodom went out to meet him at the Valley of Shaveh (that is, the King's Valley). ¶18 And King Melchizedek of Salem brought out bread and wine; he was priest of God Most High. ¶19 He blessed him and said, *"Blessed be Abram by God Most High, maker of heaven and earth; ¶20 and blessed be God Most High, who has delivered your enemies into your hand!"* And Abram

gave him one tenth of everything. ¶21 Then the king of Sodom said to Abram, "Give me the persons, but take the goods for yourself." ¶22 But Abram said to the king of Sodom, "I have sworn to the LORD, God Most High, maker of heaven and earth, ¶23 that I would not take a thread or a sandal-thong or anything that is yours, so that you might not say, 'I have made Abram rich.' ¶24 I will take nothing but what the young men have eaten, and the share of the men who went with me— Aner, Eshcol, and Mamre. Let them take their share."

15 ¶1 After these things the word of the LORD came to Abram in a vision, "Do not be afraid, Abram, I am your shield; your reward shall be very great." ¶2 But Abram said, "O Lord GOD, what will you give me, for I continue childless, and the heir of my house is Eliezer of Damascus?" ¶3 And Abram said, "You have given me no offspring, and so a slave born in my house is to be my heir." ¶ But the word of the LORD came to him, "This man shall not be your heir; no one but your very own issue shall be your heir. ¶5 He brought him outside and said, "Look toward heaven and count the stars, if you are able to count them." Then he said to him, "So shall your descendants be." ¶ And he believed the LORD; and the LORD reckoned it to him as righteousness. ¶ Then he said to him, "I am the LORD who brought you from Ur of the Chaldeans, to give you this land to possess." ¶8 But he said, "O Lord GOD, how am I to know that I shall possess it?" ¶9 He said to him, "Bring me a heifer three years old, a female

goat three years old, a ram three years old, a turtledove, and a young pigeon." ¶10 He brought him all these and cut them in two, laying each half over against the other; but he did not cut the birds in two. ¶11 And when birds of prey came down on the carcasses, Abram drove them away ¶12 As the sun was going down, a deep sleep fell upon Abram, and a deep and terrifying darkness descended upon him. ¶13 Then the LORD said to Abram, "Know this for certain, that your offspring shall be aliens in a land that is not theirs, and shall be slaves there, and they shall be oppressed for four hundred years; ¶14 but I will bring judgment on the nation that they serve, and afterward they shall come out with great possessions. ¶15 As for yourself, you shall go to your ancestors in peace; you shall be buried in a good old age. ¶16 And they shall come back here in the fourth generation; for the iniquity of the Amorites is not yet complete." ¶17 When the sun had gone down and it was dark, a smoking fire pot and a flaming torch passed between these pieces. ¶18 On that day the LORD made a covenant with Abram, saying, "To your descendants I give this land, from the river of Egypt to the great river, the river Euphrates, ¶19 the land of the Kenites, the Kenizzites, the Kadmonites, ¶20 the Hittites, the Perizzites, the Rephaim, ¶21 the Amorites, the Canaanites, the Girgashites, and the Jebusites."

16 ¶1 Now Sarai, Abram's wife, bore him no children. She had an Egyptian slave-girl whose name was Hagar, ¶2 and Sarai said to Abram,

"You see that the LORD has prevented me from bearing children; go in to my slave-girl; it may be that I shall obtain children by her." And Abram listened to the voice of Sarai. ¶3 So, after Abram had lived ten years in the land of Canaan, Sarai, Abram's wife, took Hagar the Egyptian, her slave-girl, and gave her to her husband Abram as a wife. ¶4 He went in to Hagar, and she conceived; and when she saw that she had conceived, she looked with contempt on her mistress. ¶5 Then Sarai said to Abram, "May the wrong done to me be on you! I gave my slave-girl to your embrace, and when she saw that she had conceived, she looked on me with contempt. May the LORD judge between you and me!" ¶6 But Abram said to Sarai, "Your slave-girl is in your power; do to her as you please." Then Sarai dealt harshly with her, and she ran away from her. ¶7 The angel of the LORD found her by a spring of water in the wilderness, the spring on the way to Shur. ¶8 And he said, "Hagar, slave-girl of Sarai, where have you come from and where are you going?" She said, "I am running away from my mistress Sarai." ¶9 The angel of the LORD said to her, "Return to your mistress, and submit to her." ¶10 The angel of the LORD also said to her, "I will so greatly multiply your offspring that they cannot be counted for multitude." ¶11 And the angel of the LORD said to her, *"Now you have conceived and shall bear a son; you shall call him Ishmael, for the LORD has given heed to your affliction. ¶12 He shall be a wild ass of a man, with his hand against everyone, and everyone's hand against him; and he shall live at odds with all his kin."* ¶13 So she named the LORD who spoke to her,

"You are El-roi"; for she said, "Have I really seen God and remained alive after seeing him?" ¶14 Therefore the well was called Beer-lahai-roi; it lies between Kadesh and Bered. ¶15 Hagar bore Abram a son; and Abram named his son, whom Hagar bore, Ishmael. ¶16 Abram was eighty-six years old when Hagar bore him Ishmael.

17 ¶1 When Abram was ninety-nine years old, the LORD appeared to Abram, and said to him, "I am God Almighty; walk before me, and be blameless. ¶2 And I will make my covenant between me and you, and will make you exceedingly numerous." ¶3 Then Abram fell on his face; and God said to him, ¶4 "As for me, this is my covenant with you: You shall be the ancestor of a multitude of nations. ¶5 No longer shall your name be Abram, but your name shall be Abraham; for I have made you the ancestor of a multitude of nations. ¶6 I will make you exceedingly fruitful; and I will make nations of you, and kings shall come from you. ¶7 I will establish my covenant between me and you, and your offspring after you throughout their generations, for an everlasting covenant, to be God to you and to your offspring after you. ¶8 And I will give to you, and to your offspring after you, the land where you are now an alien, all the land of Canaan, for a perpetual holding; and I will be their God." ¶9 God said to Abraham, "As for you, you shall keep my covenant, you and your offspring after you throughout their generations. ¶10 This is my covenant, which you shall keep, between me and you and your offspring

after you: Every male among you shall be circumcised. ¶11 You shall circumcise the flesh of your foreskins, and it shall be a sign of the covenant between me and you. ¶12 Throughout your generations every male among you shall be circumcised when he is eight days old, including the slave born in your house and the one bought with your money from any foreigner who is not of your offspring. ¶13 Both the slave born in your house and the one bought with your money must be circumcised. So shall my covenant be in your flesh an everlasting covenant. ¶14 Any uncircumcised male who is not circumcised in the flesh of his foreskin shall be cut off from his people; he has broken my covenant." ¶15 God said to Abraham, "As for Sarai your wife, you shall not call her Sarai, but Sarah shall be her name. ¶16 I will bless her, and moreover I will give you a son by her. I will bless her, and she shall give rise to nations; kings of peoples shall come from her." ¶17 Then Abraham fell on his face and laughed, and said to himself, "Can a child be born to a man who is a hundred years old? Can Sarah, who is ninety years old, bear a child?" ¶18 And Abraham said to God, "O that Ishmael might live in your sight!" ¶19 God said, "No, but your wife Sarah shall bear you a son, and you shall name him Isaac. I will establish my covenant with him as an everlasting covenant for his offspring after him. ¶20 As for Ishmael, I have heard you; I will bless him and make him fruitful and exceedingly numerous; he shall be the father of twelve princes, and I will make him a great nation. ¶21 But my covenant I will establish with Isaac, whom Sarah shall bear to you at this season next year." ¶22 And when he had finished talking with him, God went up from Abraham. ¶23 Then Abraham took his son Ishmael and all the slaves born in his house or bought with his money, every male among the men of Abraham's house, and he circumcised the flesh of their foreskins that very day, as God had said to him. ¶24 Abraham was ninety-nine years old when he was circumcised in the flesh of his foreskin. ¶25 And his son Ishmael was thirteen years old when he was circumcised in the flesh of his foreskin. ¶26 That very day Abraham and his son Ishmael were circumcised; ¶27 and all the men of his house, slaves born in the house and those bought with money from a foreigner, were circumcised with him.

18 ¶1 The LORD appeared to Abraham by the oaks of Mamre, as he sat at the entrance of his tent in the heat of the day. ¶2 He looked up and saw three men standing near him. When he saw them, he ran from the tent entrance to meet them, and bowed down to the ground. ¶3 He said, "My lord, if I find favor with you, do not pass by your servant. ¶4 Let a little water be brought, and wash your feet, and rest yourselves under the tree. ¶5 Let me bring a little bread, that you may refresh yourselves, and after that you may pass on—since you have come to your servant." So they said, "Do as you have said." ¶6 And Abraham hastened into the tent to Sarah, and said, "Make ready quickly three measures of choice flour, knead it, and make cakes." ¶7 Abraham ran to the herd, and took a calf, tender

and good, and gave it to the servant, who hastened to prepare it. ¶8 Then he took curds and milk and the calf that he had prepared, and set it before them; and he stood by them under the tree while they ate. ¶9 They said to him, "Where is your wife Sarah?" And he said, "There, in the tent." ¶10 Then one said, "I will surely return to you in due season, and your wife Sarah shall have a son." And Sarah was listening at the tent entrance behind him. ¶11 Now Abraham and Sarah were old, advanced in age; it had ceased to be with Sarah after the manner of women. ¶12 So Sarah laughed to herself, saying, "After I have grown old, and my husband is old, shall I have pleasure?" ¶13 The LORD said to Abraham, "Why did Sarah laugh, and say, 'Shall I indeed bear a child, now that I am old?' ¶14 Is anything too wonderful for the LORD? At the set time I will return to you, in due season, and Sarah shall have a son." ¶15 But Sarah denied, saying, "I did not laugh"; for she was afraid. He said, "Oh yes, you did laugh." ¶16 Then the men set out from there, and they looked toward Sodom; and Abraham went with them to set them on their way. ¶17 The LORD said, "Shall I hide from Abraham what I am about to do, ¶18 seeing that Abraham shall become a great and mighty nation, and all the nations of the earth shall be blessed in him? ¶19 No, for I have chosen him, that he may charge his children and his household after him to keep the way of the LORD by doing righteousness and justice; so that the LORD may bring about for Abraham what he has promised him." ¶20 Then the LORD said, "How great is the outcry against Sodom and Gomorrah and how very grave their sin! ¶21 I must go down and see whether they have done altogether according to the outcry that has come to me; and if not, I will know." ¶22 So the men turned from there, and went toward Sodom, while Abraham remained standing before the LORD. ¶23 Then Abraham came near and said, "Will you indeed sweep away the righteous with the wicked? ¶24 Suppose there are fifty righteous within the city; will you then sweep away the place and not forgive it for the fifty righteous who are in it? ¶25 Far be it from you to do such a thing, to slay the righteous with the wicked, so that the righteous fare as the wicked! Far be that from you! Shall not the Judge of all the earth do what is just?" ¶26 And the LORD said, "If I find at Sodom fifty righteous in the city, I will forgive the whole place for their sake." ¶27 Abraham answered, "Let me take it upon myself to speak to the Lord, I who am but dust and ashes. ¶28 Suppose five of the fifty righteous are lacking? Will you destroy the whole city for lack of five?" And he said, "I will not destroy it if I find forty-five there." ¶29 Again he spoke to him, "Suppose forty are found there." He answered, "For the sake of forty I will not do it." ¶30 Then he said, "Oh do not let the Lord be angry if I speak. Suppose thirty are found there." He answered, "I will not do it, if I find thirty there." ¶31 He said, "Let me take it upon myself to speak to the Lord. Suppose twenty are found there." He answered, "For the sake of twenty I will not destroy it." ¶32 Then he said, "Oh do not let the Lord be angry if I speak just once more. Suppose ten are found there." He answered, "For the sake of ten I will not destroy it." ¶33 And the LORD went his way, when he had finished speaking to Abraham; and Abraham returned to his place.

19 ¶1 The two angels came to Sodom in the evening, and Lot was sitting in the gateway of Sodom. When Lot saw them, he rose to meet them, and bowed down with his face to the ground. ¶2 He said, "Please, my lords, turn aside to your servant's house and spend the night, and wash your feet; then you can rise early and go on your way." They said, "No; we will spend the night in the square." ¶3 But he urged them strongly; so they turned aside to him and entered his house; and he made them a feast, and baked unleavened bread, and they ate. ¶4 But before they lay down, the men of the city, the men of Sodom, both young and old, all the people to the last man, surrounded the house; ¶5 and they called to Lot, "Where are the men who came to you tonight? Bring them out to us, so that we may know them." ¶6 Lot went out of the door to the men, shut the door after him, ¶7 and said, "I beg you, my brothers, do not act so wickedly. ¶8 Look, I have two daughters who have not known a man; let me bring them out to you, and do to them as you please; only do nothing to these men, for they have come under the shelter of my roof." ¶9 But they replied, "Stand back!" And they said, "This fellow came here as an alien, and he would play the judge! Now we will deal worse with you than with them." Then they pressed hard against the man Lot, and came near the door to break it down.

Chapter 19

¶10 But the men inside reached out their hands and brought Lot into the house with them, and shut the door. ¶11 And they struck with blindness the men who were at the door of the house, both small and great, so that they were unable to find the door. ¶12 Then the men said to Lot, "Have you anyone else here? Sons-in-law, sons, daughters, or anyone you have in the city—bring them out of the place. ¶13 For we are about to destroy this place, because the outcry against its people has become great before the LORD, and the LORD has sent us to destroy it." ¶14 So Lot went out and said to his sons-in-law, who were to marry his daughters, "Up, get out of this place; for the LORD is about to destroy the city." But he seemed to his sons-in-law to be jesting. ¶15 When morning dawned, the angels urged Lot, saying, "Get up, take your wife and your two daughters who are here, or else you will be consumed in the punishment of the city." ¶16 But he lingered; so the men seized him and his wife and his two daughters by the hand, the LORD being merciful to him, and they brought him out and left him outside the city. ¶17 When they had brought them outside, they said, "Flee for your life; do not look back or stop anywhere in the Plain; flee to the hills, or else you will be consumed." ¶18 And Lot said to them, "Oh, no, my lords; ¶19 your servant has found favor with you, and you have shown me great kindness in saving my life; but I cannot flee to the hills, for fear the disaster will overtake me and I die. ¶20 Look, that city is near enough to flee to, and it is a little one. Let me escape there—is it not a little one?—and my life will be saved!" ¶21 He said to him, "Very

well, I grant you this favor too, and will not overthrow the city of which you have spoken. ¶22 Hurry, escape there, for I can do nothing until you arrive there." Therefore the city was called Zoar. ¶23 The sun had risen on the earth when Lot came to Zoar. ¶24 Then the LORD rained on Sodom and Gomorrah sulfur and fire from the LORD out of heaven; ¶25 and he overthrew those cities, and all the Plain, and all the inhabitants of the cities, and what grew on the ground. ¶26 But Lot's wife, behind him, looked back, and she became a pillar of salt. ¶27 Abraham went early in the morning to the place where he had stood before the LORD; ¶28 and he looked down toward Sodom and Gomorrah and toward all the land of the Plain and saw the smoke of the land going up like the smoke of a furnace. ¶29 So it was that, when God destroyed the cities of the Plain, God remembered Abraham, and sent Lot out of the midst of the overthrow, when he overthrew the cities in which Lot had settled. ¶30 Now Lot went up out of Zoar and settled in the hills with his two daughters, for he was afraid to stay in Zoar; so he lived in a cave with his two daughters. ¶31 And the firstborn said to the younger, "Our father is old, and there is not a man on earth to come in to us after the manner of all the world. ¶32 Come, let us make our father drink wine, and we will lie with him, so that we may preserve offspring through our father." ¶33 So they made their father drink wine that night; and the firstborn went in, and lay with her father; he did not know when she lay down or when she rose. ¶34 On the next day, the firstborn said to the younger, "Look, I lay last night with my father; let us make him drink wine tonight also; then you go in and lie with him, so that we may preserve offspring through our father." ¶35 So they made their father drink wine that night also; and the younger rose, and lay with him; and he did not know when she lay down or when she rose. ¶36 Thus both the daughters of Lot became pregnant by their father. ¶37 The firstborn bore a son, and named him Moab; he is the ancestor of the Moabites to this day. ¶38 The younger also bore a son and named him Ben-ammi; he is the ancestor of the Ammonites to this day.

20 ¶1 From there Abraham journeyed toward the region of the Negeb, and settled between Kadesh and Shur. While residing in Gerar as an alien, ¶2 Abraham said of his wife Sarah, "She is my sister." And King Abimelech of Gerar sent and took Sarah. ¶3 But God came to Abimelech in a dream by night, and said to him, "You are about to die because of the woman whom you have taken; for she is a married woman." ¶4 Now Abimelech had not approached her; so he said, "Lord, will you destroy an innocent people? ¶5 Did he not himself say to me, 'She is my sister'? And she herself said, 'He is my brother.' I did this in the integrity of my heart and the innocence of my hands." ¶6 Then God said to him in the dream, "Yes, I know that you did this in the integrity of your heart; furthermore it was I who kept you from sinning against me. Therefore I did not let you touch her. ¶7 Now then, return the man's wife; for he is a prophet, and he will pray for you and

you shall live. But if you do not restore her, know that you shall surely die, you and all that are yours." ¶8 So Abimelech rose early in the morning, and called all his servants and told them all these things; and the men were very much afraid. ¶9 Then Abimelech called Abraham, and said to him, "What have you done to us? How have I sinned against you, that you have brought such great guilt on me and my kingdom? You have done things to me that ought not to be done." ¶10 And Abimelech said to Abraham, "What were you thinking of, that you did this thing?" ¶11 Abraham said, "I did it because I thought, There is no fear of God at all in this place, and they will kill me because of my wife. ¶12 Besides, she is indeed my sister, the daughter of my father but not the daughter of my mother; and she became my wife. ¶13 And when God caused me to wander from my father's house, I said to her, 'This is the kindness you must do me: at every place to which we come, say of me, He is my brother.'" ¶14 Then Abimelech took sheep and oxen, and male and female slaves, and gave them to Abraham, and restored his wife Sarah to him. ¶15 Abimelech said, "My land is before you; settle where it pleases you." ¶16 To Sarah he said, "Look, I have given your brother a thousand pieces of silver; it is your exoneration before all who are with you; you are completely vindicated." ¶17 Then Abraham prayed to God; and God healed Abimelech, and also healed his wife and female slaves so that they bore children. ¶18 For the LORD had closed fast all the wombs of the house of Abimelech because of Sarah, Abraham's wife.

21

¶1 The LORD dealt with Sarah as he had said, and the LORD did for Sarah as he had promised. ¶2 Sarah conceived and bore Abraham a son in his old age, at the time of which God had spoken to him. ¶3 Abraham gave the name Isaac to his son whom Sarah bore him. ¶4 And Abraham circumcised his son Isaac when he was eight days old, as God had commanded him. ¶5 Abraham was a hundred years old when his son Isaac was born to him. ¶6 Now Sarah said, "God has brought laughter for me; everyone who hears will laugh with me." ¶7 And she said, "Who would ever have said to Abraham that Sarah would nurse children? Yet I have borne him a son in his old age." ¶8 The child grew, and was weaned; and Abraham made a great feast on the day that Isaac was weaned. ¶9 But Sarah saw the son of Hagar the Egyptian, whom she had borne to Abraham, playing with her son Isaac. ¶10 So she said to Abraham, "Cast out this slave woman with her son; for the son of this slave woman shall not inherit along with my son Isaac." ¶11 The matter was very distressing to Abraham on account of his son. ¶12 But God said to Abraham, "Do not be distressed because of the boy and because of your slave woman; whatever Sarah says to you, do as she tells you, for it is through Isaac that offspring shall be named for you. ¶13 As for the son of the slave woman, I will make a nation of him also, because he is your offspring." ¶14 So Abraham rose early in the morning, and took bread and a skin of water, and gave it to Hagar, putting it on her shoulder, along with the child, and sent her away. And she departed, and wandered about in the wilderness of Beer-sheba. ¶15 When the water in the skin was gone, she cast the child under one of the bushes. ¶16 Then she went and sat down opposite him a good way off, about the distance of a bowshot; for she said, "Do not let me look on the death of the child." And as she sat opposite him, she lifted up her voice and wept. ¶17 And God heard the voice of the boy; and the angel of God called to Hagar from heaven, and said to her, "What troubles you, Hagar? Do not be afraid; for God has heard the voice of the boy where he is. ¶18 Come, lift up the boy and hold him fast with your hand, for I will make a great nation of him." ¶19 Then God opened her eyes and she saw a well of water. She went, and filled the skin with water, and gave the boy a drink. ¶20 God was with the boy, and he grew up; he lived in the wilderness, and became an expert with the bow. ¶21 He lived in the wilderness of Paran; and his mother got a wife for him from the land of Egypt. ¶22 At that time Abimelech, with Phicol the commander of his army, said to Abraham, "God is with you in all that you do; ¶23 now therefore swear to me here by God that you will not deal falsely with me or with my offspring or with my posterity, but as I have dealt loyally with you, you will deal with me and with the land where you have resided as an alien." ¶24 And Abraham said, "I swear it." ¶25 When Abraham complained to Abimelech about a well of water that Abimelech's servants had seized, ¶26 Abimelech said, "I do not know who has done this; you did not tell me, and I have not heard of it until today." ¶27 So Abraham took sheep and oxen and gave them to

Abimelech, and the two men made a covenant. ¶28 Abraham set apart seven ewe lambs of the flock. ¶29 And Abimelech said to Abraham, "What is the meaning of these seven ewe lambs that you have set apart?" ¶30 He said, "These seven ewe lambs you shall accept from my hand, in order that you may be a witness for me that I dug this well." ¶31 Therefore that place was called Beer-sheba; because there both of them swore an oath. ¶32 When they had made a covenant at Beer-sheba, Abimelech, with Phicol the commander of his army, left and returned to the land of the Philistines. ¶33 Abraham planted a tamarisk tree in Beer-sheba, and called there on the name of the LORD, the Everlasting God. ¶34 And Abraham resided as an alien many days in the land of the Philistines.

22 ¶1 After these things God tested Abraham. He said to him, "Abraham!" And he said, "Here I am." ¶2 He said, "Take your son, your only son Isaac, whom you love, and go to the land of Moriah, and offer him there as a burnt offering on one of the mountains that I shall show you." ¶3 So Abraham rose early in the morning, saddled his donkey, and took two of his young men with him, and his son Isaac; he cut the wood for the burnt offering, and set out and went to the place in the distance that God had shown him. ¶4 On the third day Abraham looked up and saw the place far away. ¶5 Then Abraham said to his young men, "Stay here with the donkey; the boy and I will go over there; we will worship, and then we will come back to you." ¶6 Abraham took the wood of the burnt offering and laid it on his son Isaac, and he himself carried the fire and the knife. So the two of them walked on together. ¶7 Isaac said to his father Abraham, "Father!" And he said, "Here I am, my son." He said, "The fire and the wood are here, but where is the lamb for a burnt offering?" ¶8 Abraham said, "God himself will provide the lamb for a burnt offering, my son." So the two of them walked on together. ¶9 When they came to the place that God had shown him, Abraham built an altar there and laid the wood in order. He bound his son Isaac, and laid him on the altar, on top of the wood. ¶10 Then Abraham reached out his hand and took the knife to kill his son. ¶11 But the angel of the LORD called to him from heaven, and said, "Abraham, Abraham!" And he said, "Here I am." ¶12 He said, "Do not lay your hand on the boy or do anything to him; for now I know that you fear God, since you have not withheld your son, your only son, from me." ¶13 And Abraham looked up and saw a ram, caught in a thicket by its horns. Abraham went and took the ram and offered it up as a burnt offering instead of his son. ¶14 So Abraham called that place "The LORD will provide"; as it is said to this day, "On the mount of the LORD it shall be provided." ¶15 The angel of the LORD called to Abraham a second time from heaven, ¶16 and said, "By myself I have sworn, says the LORD: Because you have done this, and have not withheld your son, your only son, ¶17 I will indeed bless you, and I will make your offspring as numerous as the stars of heaven and as the sand that is on the

seashore. And your offspring shall possess the gate of their enemies, ¶18 and by your offspring shall all the nations of the earth gain blessing for themselves, because you have obeyed my voice." ¶19 So Abraham returned to his young men, and they arose and went together to Beer-sheba; and Abraham lived at Beer-sheba. ¶20 Now after these things it was told Abraham, "Milcah also has borne children, to your brother Nahor: ¶21 Uz the firstborn, Buz his brother, Kemuel the father of Aram, ¶22 Chesed, Hazo, Pildash, Jidlaph, and Bethuel." ¶23 Bethuel became the father of Rebekah. These eight Milcah bore to Nahor, Abraham's brother. ¶24 Moreover, his concubine, whose name was Reumah, bore Tebah, Gaham, Tahash, and Maacah.

23 ¶1 Sarah lived one hundred twenty-seven years; this was the length of Sarah's life. ¶2 And Sarah died at Kiriath-arba (that is, Hebron) in the land of Canaan; and Abraham went in to mourn for Sarah and to weep for her. ¶3 Abraham rose up from beside his dead, and said to the Hittites, ¶4 "I am a stranger and an alien residing among you; give me property among you for a burying place, so that I may bury my dead out of my sight." ¶5 The Hittites answered Abraham, ¶6 "Hear us, my lord; you are a mighty prince among us. Bury your dead in the choicest of our burial places; none of us will withhold from you any burial ground for burying your dead." ¶7 Abraham rose and bowed to the Hittites, the people of the land. ¶8 He said to them,

"If you are willing that I should bury my dead out of my sight, hear me, and entreat for me Ephron son of Zohar, ¶9 so that he may give me the cave of Machpelah, which he owns; it is at the end of his field. For the full price let him give it to me in your presence as a possession for a burying place." ¶10 Now Ephron was sitting among the Hittites; and Ephron the Hittite answered Abraham in the hearing of the Hittites, of all who went in at the gate of his city, ¶11 "No, my lord, hear me; I give you the field, and I give you the cave that is in it; in the presence of my people I give it to you; bury your dead." ¶12 Then Abraham bowed down before the people of the land. ¶13 He said to Ephron in the hearing of the people of the land, "If you only will listen to me! I will give the price of the field; accept it from me, so that I may bury my dead there." ¶14 Ephron answered Abraham, ¶15 "My lord, listen to me; a piece of land worth four hundred shekels of silver—what is that between you and me? Bury your dead." ¶16 Abraham agreed with Ephron; and Abraham weighed out for Ephron the silver that he had named in the hearing of the Hittites, four hundred shekels of silver, according to the weights current among the merchants. ¶17 So the field of Ephron in Machpelah, which was to the east of Mamre, the field with the cave that was in it and all the trees that were in the field, throughout its whole area, passed ¶18 to Abraham as a possession in the presence of the Hittites, in the presence of all who went in at the gate of his city. ¶19 After this, Abraham buried Sarah his wife in the cave of the field of Machpelah facing Mamre (that is, Hebron) in the land of

Canaan. ¶20 The field and the cave that is in it passed from the Hittites into Abraham's possession as a burying place.

24 ¶1 Now Abraham was old, well advanced in years; and the LORD had blessed Abraham in all things. ¶2 Abraham said to his servant, the oldest of his house, who had charge of all that he had, "Put your hand under my thigh ¶3 and I will make you swear by the LORD, the God of heaven and earth, that you will not get a wife for my son from the daughters of the Canaanites, among whom I live, ¶4 but will go to my country and to my kindred and get a wife for my son Isaac." ¶5 The servant said to him, "Perhaps the woman may not be willing to follow me to this land; must I then take your son back to the land from which you came?" ¶6 Abraham said to him, "See to it that you do not take my son back there. ¶7 The LORD, the God of heaven, who took me from my father's house and from the land of my birth, and who spoke to me and swore to me, 'To your offspring I will give this land,' he will send his angel before you, and you shall take a wife for my son from there. ¶8 But if the woman is not willing to follow you, then you will be free from this oath of mine; only you must not take my son back there." ¶9 So the servant put his hand under the thigh of Abraham his master and swore to him concerning this matter. ¶10 Then the servant took ten of his master's camels and departed, taking all kinds of choice gifts from his master; and he set out and went to Aramnaharaim, to the city of Nahor.

¶11 He made the camels kneel down outside the city by the well of water; it was toward evening, the time when women go out to draw water. ¶12 And he said, "O LORD, God of my master Abraham, please grant me success today and show steadfast love to my master Abraham. ¶13 I am standing here by the spring of water, and the daughters of the townspeople are coming out to draw water. ¶14 Let the girl to whom I shall say, 'Please offer your jar that I may drink,' and who shall say, 'Drink, and I will water your camels'—let her be the one whom you have appointed for your servant Isaac. By this I shall know that you have shown steadfast love to my master." ¶15 Before he had finished speaking, there was Rebekah, who was born to Bethuel son of Milcah, the wife of Nahor, Abraham's brother, coming out with her water jar on her shoulder. ¶16 The girl was very fair to look upon, a virgin, whom no man had known. She went down to the spring, filled her jar, and came up. ¶17 Then the servant ran to meet her and said, "Please let me sip a little water from your jar." ¶18 "Drink, my lord," she said, and quickly lowered her jar upon her hand and gave him a drink. ¶19 When she had finished giving him a drink, she said, "I will draw for your camels also, until they have finished drinking." ¶20 So she quickly emptied her jar into the trough and ran again to the well to draw, and she drew for all his camels. ¶21 The man gazed at her in silence to learn whether or not the LORD had made his journey successful. ¶22 When the camels had finished drinking, the man took a gold nose-ring weighing a half shekel, and two bracelets for her arms weighing ten gold shekels, ¶23 and said, "Tell me whose daughter you are. Is there room in your father's house for us to spend the night?" ¶24 She said to him, "I am the daughter of Bethuel son of Milcah, whom she bore to Nahor." ¶25 She added, "We have plenty of straw and fodder and a place to spend the night." ¶26 The man bowed his head and worshiped the LORD ¶27 and said, "Blessed be the LORD, the God of my master Abraham, who has not forsaken his steadfast love and his faithfulness toward my master. As for me, the LORD has led me on the way to the house of my master's kin." ¶28 Then the girl ran and told her mother's household about these things. ¶29 Rebekah had a brother whose name was Laban; and Laban ran out to the man, to the spring. ¶30 As soon as he had seen the nose-ring, and the bracelets on his sister's arms, and when he heard the words of his sister Rebekah, "Thus the man spoke to me," he went to the man; and there he was, standing by the camels at the spring. ¶31 He said, "Come in, O blessed of the LORD. Why do you stand outside when I have prepared the house and a place for the camels?" ¶32 So the man came into the house; and Laban unloaded the camels, and gave him straw and fodder for the camels, and water to wash his feet and the feet of the men who were with him. ¶33 Then food was set before him to eat; but he said, "I will not eat until I have told my errand." He said, "Speak on." ¶34 So he said, "I am Abraham's servant. ¶35 The LORD has greatly blessed my master, and he has become wealthy; he has given him flocks and herds, silver and gold, male and female slaves, camels and donkeys. ¶36 And Sarah my master's wife bore a son to my master when she was old; and he has given him all that he has. ¶37 My master made me swear, saying, 'You shall not take a wife for my son from the daughters of the Canaanites, in whose land I live; ¶38 but you shall go to my father's house, to my kindred, and get a wife for my son.' ¶39 I said to my master, 'Perhaps the woman will not follow me.' ¶40 But he said to me, 'The LORD, before whom I walk, will send his angel with you and make your way successful. You shall get a wife for my son from my kindred, from my father's house. ¶41 Then you will be free from my oath, when you come to my kindred; even if they will not give her to you, you will be free from my oath.' ¶42 "I came today to the spring, and said, 'O LORD, the God of my master Abraham, if now you will only make successful the way I am going! ¶43 I am standing here by the spring of water; let the young woman who comes out to draw, to whom I shall say, "Please give me a little water from your jar to drink," ¶44 and who will say to me, "Drink, and I will draw for your camels also"—let her be the woman whom the LORD has appointed for my master's son.' ¶45 "Before I had finished speaking in my heart, there was Rebekah coming out with her water jar on her shoulder; and she went down to the spring, and drew. I said to her, 'Please let me drink.' ¶46 She quickly let down her jar from her shoulder, and said, 'Drink, and I will also water your camels.' So I drank, and she also watered the camels. ¶47 Then I asked her, 'Whose daughter are you?' She said, 'The daughter of Bethuel, Nahor's son, whom Milcah bore to him.' So I put the ring on her nose, and the bracelets on her arms. ¶48 Then I bowed my head and worshiped the LORD, and blessed the LORD, the God of my master Abraham, who had led me by the right way to obtain the daughter of my master's kinsman for his son. ¶49 Now then, if you will deal loyally and truly with my master, tell me; and if not, tell me, so that I may turn either to the right hand or to the left." ¶50 Then Laban and Bethuel answered, "The thing comes from the LORD; we cannot speak to you anything bad or good. ¶51 Look, Rebekah is before you, take her and go, and let her be the wife of your master's son, as the LORD has spoken." ¶52 When Abraham's servant heard their words, he bowed himself to the ground before the LORD. ¶53 And the servant brought out jewelry of silver and of gold, and garments, and gave them to Rebekah; he also gave to her brother and to her mother costly ornaments. ¶54 Then he and the men who were with him ate and drank, and they spent the night there. When they rose in the morning, he said, "Send me back to my master." ¶55 Her brother and her mother said, "Let the girl remain with us a while, at least ten days; after that she may go." ¶56 But he said to them, "Do not delay me, since the LORD has made my journey successful; let me go that I may go to my master." ¶57 They said, "We will call the girl, and ask her." ¶58 And they called Rebekah, and said to her, "Will you go with this man?" She said, "I will." ¶59 So they sent away their sister Rebekah and her nurse along with Abraham's servant and his men. ¶60 And they blessed Rebekah and said to her, *"May you, our sister, become thousands of myriads; may your offspring gain possession of the gates of their foes."* ¶61 Then Rebekah and her maids rose up, mounted the camels, and followed the man; thus the servant took Rebekah, and went his way. ¶62 Now Isaac had come from Beer-lahai-roi, and was settled in the Negeb. ¶63 Isaac went out in the evening to walk in the field; and looking up, he saw camels coming. ¶64 And Rebekah looked up, and when she saw Isaac, she slipped quickly from the camel, ¶65 and said to the servant, "Who is the man over there, walking in the field to meet us?" The servant said, "It is my master." So she took her veil and covered herself. ¶66 And the servant told Isaac all the things that he had done. ¶67 Then Isaac brought her into his mother Sarah's tent. He took Rebekah, and she became his wife; and he loved her. So Isaac was comforted after his mother's death.

25 ¶1 Abraham took another wife, whose name was Keturah. ¶2 She bore him Zimran, Jokshan, Medan, Midian, Ishbak, and Shuah. ¶3 Jokshan was the father of Sheba and Dedan. The sons of Dedan were Asshurim, Letushim, and Leummim. ¶4 The sons of Midian were Ephah, Epher, Hanoch, Abida, and Eldaah. All these were the children of Keturah. ¶5 Abraham gave all he had to Isaac. ¶6 But to the sons of his concubines Abraham gave gifts, while he was still living, and he sent them away from his son Isaac, eastward to the east country. ¶7 This is the length of Abraham's life, one hundred seventy-five years. ¶8 Abraham breathed his last and died in a good old age,

an old man and full of years, and was gathered to his people. ¶9 His sons Isaac and Ishmael buried him in the cave of Machpelah, in the field of Ephron son of Zohar the Hittite, east of Mamre, ¶10 the field that Abraham purchased from the Hittites. There Abraham was buried, with his wife Sarah. ¶11 After the death of Abraham God blessed his son Isaac. And Isaac settled at Beer-lahai-roi. ¶12 These are the descendants of Ishmael, Abraham's son, whom Hagar the Egyptian, Sarah's slave-girl, bore to Abraham. ¶13 These are the names of the sons of Ishmael, named in the order of their birth: Nebaioth, the firstborn of Ishmael; and Kedar, Adbeel, Mibsam, ¶14 Mishma, Dumah, Massa, ¶15 Hadad, Tema, Jetur, Naphish, and Kedemah. ¶16 These are the sons of Ishmael and these are their names, by their villages and by their encampments, twelve princes according to their tribes. ¶17 (This is the length of the life of Ishmael, one hundred thirty-seven years; he breathed his last and died, and was gathered to his people.) ¶18 They settled from Havilah to Shur, which is opposite Egypt in the direction of Assyria; he settled down alongside of all his people. ¶19 These are the descendants of Isaac, Abraham's son: Abraham was the father of Isaac, ¶20 and Isaac was forty years old when he married Rebekah, daughter of Bethuel the Aramean of Paddan-aram, sister of Laban the Aramean. ¶21 Isaac prayed to the LORD for his wife, because she was barren; and the LORD granted his prayer, and his wife Rebekah conceived. ¶22 The children struggled together within her; and she said, "If it is to be this way, why do I live?" So she went to inquire of the

LORD. ¶23 And the LORD said to her, *"Two nations are in your womb, and two peoples born of you shall be divided; the one shall be stronger than the other, the elder shall serve the younger."* ¶24 When her time to give birth was at hand, there were twins in her womb. ¶25 The first came out red, all his body like a hairy mantle; so they named him Esau. ¶26 Afterward his brother came out, with his hand gripping Esau's heel; so he was named Jacob. Isaac was sixty years old when she bore them. ¶27 When the boys grew up, Esau was a skillful hunter, a man of the field, while Jacob was a quiet man, living in tents. ¶28 Isaac loved Esau, because he was fond of game; but Rebekah loved Jacob. ¶29 Once when Jacob was cooking a stew, Esau came in from the field, and he was famished. ¶30 Esau said to Jacob, "Let me eat some of that red stuff, for I am famished!" (Therefore he was called Edom.) ¶31 Jacob said, "First sell me your birthright." ¶32 Esau said, "I am about to die; of what use is a birthright to me?" ¶33 Jacob said, "Swear to me first." So he swore to him, and sold his birthright to Jacob. ¶34 Then Jacob gave Esau bread and lentil stew, and he ate and drank, and rose and went his way. Thus Esau despised his birthright.

26

¶1 Now there was a famine in the land, besides the former famine that had occurred in the days of Abraham. And Isaac went to Gerar, to King Abimelech of the Philistines. ¶2 The LORD appeared to Isaac and said, "Do not go down to Egypt; settle in the land that I shall show you. ¶3 Reside in this land as an alien, and I will be with you, and will bless you; for to you and to your descendants I will give all these lands, and I will fulfill the oath that I swore to your father Abraham. ¶4 I will make your offspring as numerous as the stars of heaven, and will give to your offspring all these lands; and all the nations of the earth shall gain blessing for themselves through your offspring, ¶5 because Abraham obeyed my voice and kept my charge, my commandments, my statutes, and my laws." ¶6 So Isaac settled in Gerar. ¶7 When the men of the place asked him about his wife, he said, "She is my sister"; for he was afraid to say, "My wife," thinking, "or else the men of the place might kill me for the sake of Rebekah, because she is attractive in appearance." ¶8 When Isaac had been there a long time, King Abimelech of the Philistines looked out of a window and saw him fondling his wife Rebekah. ¶9 So Abimelech called for Isaac, and said, "So she is your wife! Why then did you say, 'She is my sister'?" Isaac said to him, "Because I thought I might die because of her." ¶10 Abimelech said, "What is this you have done to us? One of the people might easily have lain with your wife, and you would have brought guilt upon us." ¶11 So Abimelech warned all the people, saying, "Whoever touches this man or his wife shall be put to death." ¶12 Isaac sowed seed in that land, and in the same year reaped a hundredfold. The LORD blessed him, ¶13 and the man became rich; he prospered more and more until he became very wealthy. ¶14 He had possessions of flocks and herds, and a great household, so that the Philistines envied him. ¶15 (Now

the Philistines had stopped up and filled with earth all the wells that his father's servants had dug in the days of his father Abraham.) ¶16 And Abimelech said to Isaac, "Go away from us; you have become too powerful for us." ¶17 So Isaac departed from there and camped in the valley of Gerar and settled there. ¶18 Isaac dug again the wells of water that had been dug in the days of his father Abraham; for the Philistines had stopped them up after the death of Abraham; and he gave them the names that his father had given them. ¶19 But when Isaac's servants dug in the valley and found there a well of spring water, ¶20 the herders of Gerar quarreled with Isaac's herders, saying, "The water is ours." So he called the well Esek, because they contended with him. ¶21 Then they dug another well, and they quarreled over that one also; so he called it Sitnah. ¶22 He moved from there and dug another well, and they did not quarrel over it; so he called it Rehoboth, saying, "Now the LORD has made room for us, and we shall be fruitful in the land." ¶23 From there he went up to Beer-sheba. ¶24 And that very night the LORD appeared to him and said, "I am the God of your father Abraham; do not be afraid, for I am with you and will bless you and make your offspring numerous for my servant Abraham's sake." ¶25 So he built an altar there, called on the name of the LORD, and pitched his tent there. And there Isaac's servants dug a well. ¶26 Then Abimelech went to him from Gerar, with Ahuzzath his adviser and Phicol the commander of his army. ¶27 Isaac said to them, "Why have you come to me, seeing that you hate me and have sent me away from you?" ¶28 They said, "We see plainly that the LORD has been with you; so we say, let there be an oath between you and us, and let us make a covenant with you ¶29 so that you will do us no harm, just as we have not touched you and have done to you nothing but good and have sent you away in peace. You are now the blessed of the LORD." ¶30 So he made them a feast, and they ate and drank. ¶31 In the morning they rose early and exchanged oaths; and Isaac set them on their way, and they departed from him in peace. ¶32 That same day Isaac's servants came and told him about the well that they had dug, and said to him, "We have found water!" ¶33 He called it Shibah; therefore the name of the city is Beer-sheba to this day. ¶34 When Esau was forty years old, he married Judith daughter of Beeri the Hittite, and Basemath daughter of Elon the Hittite; ¶35 and they made life bitter for Isaac and Rebekah.

27 ¶1 When Isaac was old and his eyes were dim so that he could not see, he called his elder son Esau and said to him, "My son"; and he answered, "Here I am." ¶2 He said, "See, I am old; I do not know the day of my death. ¶3 Now then, take your weapons, your quiver and your bow, and go out to the field, and hunt game for me. ¶4 Then prepare for me savory food, such as I like, and bring it to me to eat, so that I may bless you before I die." ¶5 Now Rebekah was listening when Isaac spoke to his son Esau. So when Esau went to the field to hunt for game and bring it, ¶6 Rebekah said to her son Jacob, "I heard your father say to your brother Esau, ¶7 'Bring me game, and prepare for me savory food to eat, that I may bless you before the LORD before I die.' ¶8 Now therefore, my son, obey my word as I command you. ¶9 Go to the flock, and get me two choice kids, so that I may prepare from them savory food for your father, such as he likes; ¶10 and you shall take it to your father to eat, so that he may bless you before he dies." ¶11 But Jacob said to his mother Rebekah, "Look, my brother Esau is a hairy man, and I am a man of smooth skin. ¶12 Perhaps my father will feel me, and I shall seem to be mocking him, and bring a curse on myself and not a blessing." ¶13 His mother said to him, "Let your curse be on me, my son; only obey my word, and go, get them for me." ¶14 So he went and got them and brought them to his mother; and his mother prepared savory food, such as his father loved. ¶15 Then Rebekah took the best garments of her elder son Esau, which were with her in the house, and put them on her younger son Jacob; ¶16 and she put the skins of the kids on his hands and on the smooth part of his neck. ¶17 Then she handed the savory food, and the bread that she had prepared, to her son Jacob. ¶18 So he went in to his father, and said, "My father"; and he said, "Here I am; who are you, my son?" ¶19 Jacob said to his father, "I am Esau your firstborn. I have done as you told me; now sit up and eat of my game, so that you may bless me." ¶20 But Isaac said to his son, "How is it that you have found it so quickly, my son?" He answered, "Because the LORD your God granted me success." ¶21 Then Isaac said to Jacob, "Come near, that I may

feel you, my son, to know whether you are really my son Esau or not." ¶22 So Jacob went up to his father Isaac, who felt him and said, "The voice is Jacob's voice, but the hands are the hands of Esau." ¶23 He did not recognize him, because his hands were hairy like his brother Esau's hands; so he blessed him. ¶24 He said, "Are you really my son Esau?" He answered, "I am." ¶25 Then he said, "Bring it to me, that I may eat of my son's game and bless you." So he brought it to him, and he ate; and he brought him wine, and he drank. ¶26 Then his father Isaac said to him, "Come near and kiss me, my son." ¶27 So he came near and kissed him; and he smelled the smell of his garments, and blessed him, and said, *"Ah, the smell of my son is like the smell of a field that the* LORD *has blessed.* ¶28 *May God give you of the dew of heaven, and of the fatness of the earth, and plenty of grain and wine.* ¶29 *Let peoples serve you, and nations bow down to you. Be lord over your brothers, and may your mother's sons bow down to you. Cursed be everyone who curses you, and blessed be everyone who blesses you!"* ¶30 As soon as Isaac had finished blessing Jacob, when Jacob had scarcely gone out from the presence of his father Isaac, his brother Esau came in from his hunting. ¶31 He also prepared savory food, and brought it to his father. And he said to his father, "Let my father sit up and eat of his son's game, so that you may bless me." ¶32 His father Isaac said to him, "Who are you?" He answered, "I am your firstborn son, Esau." ¶33 Then Isaac trembled violently, and said, "Who was it then that hunted game and brought it to me, and I

ate it all before you came, and I have blessed him?—yes, and blessed he shall be!" ¶34 When Esau heard his father's words, he cried out with an exceedingly great and bitter cry, and said to his father, "Bless me, me also, father!" ¶35 But he said, "Your brother came deceitfully, and he has taken away your blessing." ¶36 Esau said, "Is he not rightly named Jacob? For he has supplanted me these two times. He took away my birthright; and look, now he has taken away my blessing." Then he said, "Have you not reserved a blessing for me?" ¶37 Isaac answered Esau, "I have already made him your lord, and I have given him all his brothers as servants, and with grain and wine I have sustained him. What then can I do for you, my son?" ¶38 Esau said to his father, "Have you only one blessing, father? Bless me, me also, father!" And Esau lifted up his voice and wept. ¶39 Then his father Isaac answered him: *"See, away from the fatness of the earth shall your home be, and away from the dew of heaven on high.* ¶40 *By your sword you shall live, and you shall serve your brother; but when you break loose, you shall break his yoke from your neck."* ¶41 Now Esau hated Jacob because of the blessing with which his father had blessed him, and Esau said to himself, "The days of mourning for my father are approaching; then I will kill my brother Jacob." ¶42 But the words of her elder son Esau were told to Rebekah; so she sent and called her younger son Jacob and said to him, "Your brother Esau is consoling himself by planning to kill you. ¶43 Now therefore, my son, obey my voice; flee at once to my brother Laban in Haran, ¶44 and stay with him a while, until your brother's fury turns away— ¶45 until your brother's anger against you turns away, and he forgets what you have done to him; then I will send, and bring you back from there. Why should I lose both of you in one day?" ¶46 Then Rebekah said to Isaac, "I am weary of my life because of the Hittite women. If Jacob marries one of the Hittite women such as these, one of the women of the land, what good will my life be to me?"

28 ¶1 Then Isaac called Jacob and blessed him, and charged him, "You shall not marry one of the Canaanite women. ¶2 Go at once to Paddan-aram to the house of Bethuel, your mother's father; and take as wife from there one of the daughters of Laban, your mother's brother. ¶3 May God Almighty bless you and make you fruitful and numerous, that you may become a company of peoples. ¶4 May he give to you the blessing of Abraham, to you and to your offspring with you, so that you may take possession of the land where you now live as an alien—land that God gave to Abraham." ¶5 Thus Isaac sent Jacob away; and he went to Paddan-aram, to Laban son of Bethuel the Aramean, the brother of Rebekah, Jacob's and Esau's mother. ¶6 Now Esau saw that Isaac had blessed Jacob and sent him away to Paddan-aram to take a wife from there, and that as he blessed him he charged him, "You shall not marry one of the Canaanite women," ¶7 and that Jacob had obeyed his father and his mother and gone to Paddan-aram. ¶8 So when Esau saw that the Canaanite women did not please his father Isaac, ¶9 Esau went to Ishmael and took Mahalath daughter of Abraham's son Ishmael, and sister of Nebaioth, to be his wife in addition to the wives he had. ¶10 Jacob left Beer-sheba and went toward Haran. ¶11 He came to a certain place and stayed there for the night, because the sun had set. Taking one of the stones of the place, he put it under his head and lay down in that place. ¶12 And he dreamed that there was a ladder set up on the earth, the top of it reaching to heaven; and the angels of God were ascending and descending on it. ¶13 And the LORD stood beside him and said, "I am the LORD, the God of Abraham your father and the God of Isaac; the land on which you lie I will give to you and to your offspring; ¶14 and your offspring shall be like the dust of the earth, and you shall spread abroad to the west and to the east and to the north and to the south; and all the families of the earth shall be blessed in you and in your offspring. ¶15 Know that I am with you and will keep you wherever you go, and will bring you back to this land; for I will not leave you until I have done what I have promised you." ¶16 Then Jacob woke from his sleep and said, "Surely the LORD is in this place—and I did not know it!" ¶17 And he was afraid, and said, "How awesome is this place! This is none other than the house of God, and this is the gate of heaven." ¶18 So Jacob rose early in the morning, and he took the stone that he had put under his head and set it up for a pillar and poured oil on the top of it. ¶19 He called that place Bethel; but the name of the city was Luz at the first. ¶20 Then Jacob made a vow, saying, "If God will be with me, and will keep me in this way that I

go, and will give me bread to eat and clothing to wear, ¶21 so that I come again to my father's house in peace, then the LORD shall be my God, ¶22 and this stone, which I have set up for a pillar, shall be God's house; and of all that you give me I will surely give one tenth to you."

29 ¶1 Then Jacob went on his journey, and came to the land of the people of the east. ¶2 As he looked, he saw a well in the field and three flocks of sheep lying there beside it; for out of that well the flocks were watered. The stone on the well's mouth was large, ¶3 and when all the flocks were gathered there, the shepherds would roll the stone from the mouth of the well, and water the sheep, and put the stone back in its place on the mouth of the well. ¶4 Jacob said to them, "My brothers, where do you come from?" They said, "We are from Haran." ¶5 He said to them, "Do you know Laban son of Nahor?" They said, "We do." ¶6 He said to them, "Is it well with him?" "Yes," they replied, "and here is his daughter Rachel, coming with the sheep." ¶7 He said, "Look, it is still broad daylight; it is not time for the animals to be gathered together. Water the sheep, and go, pasture them." ¶8 But they said, "We cannot until all the flocks are gathered together, and the stone is rolled from the mouth of the well; then we water the sheep." ¶9 While he was still speaking with them, Rachel came with her father's sheep; for she kept them. ¶10 Now when Jacob saw Rachel, the daughter of his mother's brother Laban, and the sheep of his mother's brother Laban, Jacob went up and rolled the stone from the well's mouth, and watered the flock of his mother's brother Laban. ¶11 Then Jacob kissed Rachel, and wept aloud. ¶12 And Jacob told Rachel that he was her father's kinsman, and that he was Rebekah's son; and she ran and told her father. ¶13 When Laban heard the news about his sister's son Jacob, he ran to meet him; he embraced him and kissed him, and brought him to his house. Jacob told Laban all these things, ¶14 and Laban said to him, "Surely you are my bone and my flesh!" And he stayed with him a month. ¶15 Then Laban said to Jacob, "Because you are my kinsman, should you therefore serve me for nothing? Tell me, what shall your wages be?" ¶16 Now Laban had two daughters; the name of the elder was Leah, and the name of the younger was Rachel. ¶17 Leah's eyes were lovely, and Rachel was graceful and beautiful. ¶18 Jacob loved Rachel; so he said, "I will serve you seven years for your younger daughter Rachel." ¶19 Laban said, "It is better that I give her to you than that I should give her to any other man; stay with me." ¶20 So Jacob served seven years for Rachel, and they seemed to him but a few days because of the love he had for her. ¶21 Then Jacob said to Laban, "Give me my wife that I may go in to her, for my time is completed." ¶22 So Laban gathered together all the people of the place, and made a feast. ¶23 But in the evening he took his daughter Leah and brought her to Jacob; and he went in to her. ¶24 (Laban gave his maid Zilpah to his daughter Leah to be her maid.) ¶25 When morning came, it was Leah! And

Jacob said to Laban, "What is this you have done to me? Did I not serve with you for Rachel? Why then have you deceived me?" ¶26 Laban said, "This is not done in our country—giving the younger before the firstborn. ¶27 Complete the week of this one, and we will give you the other also in return for serving me another seven years." ¶28 Jacob did so, and completed her week; then Laban gave him his daughter Rachel as a wife. ¶29 (Laban gave his maid Bilhah to his daughter Rachel to be her maid.) ¶30 So Jacob went in to Rachel also, and he loved Rachel more than Leah. He served Laban for another seven years. ¶31 When the LORD saw that Leah was unloved, he opened her womb; but Rachel was barren. ¶32 Leah conceived and bore a son, and she named him Reuben; for she said, "Because the LORD has looked on my affliction; surely now my husband will love me." ¶33 She conceived again and bore a son, and said, "Because the LORD has heard that I am hated, he has given me this son also"; and she named him Simeon. ¶34 Again she conceived and bore a son, and said, "Now this time my husband will be joined to me, because I have borne him three sons"; therefore he was named Levi. ¶35 She conceived again and bore a son, and said, "This time I will praise the LORD"; therefore she named him Judah; then she ceased bearing.

30 ¶1 When Rachel saw that she bore Jacob no children, she envied her sister; and she said to Jacob, "Give me children, or I shall die!" ¶2 Jacob became very angry with Rachel and said, "Am I in the place of God, who has withheld from you the fruit of the womb?" ¶3 Then she said, "Here is my maid Bilhah; go in to her, that she may bear upon my knees and that I too may have children through her." ¶4 So she gave him her maid Bilhah as a wife; and Jacob went in to her. ¶5 And Bilhah conceived and bore Jacob a son. ¶6 Then Rachel said, "God has judged me, and has also heard my voice and given me a son"; therefore she named him Dan. ¶7 Rachel's maid Bilhah conceived again and bore Jacob a second son. ¶8 Then Rachel said, "With mighty wrestlings I have wrestled with my sister, and have prevailed"; so she named him Naphtali. ¶9 When Leah saw that she had ceased bearing children, she took her maid Zilpah and gave her to Jacob as a wife. ¶10 Then Leah's maid Zilpah bore Jacob a son. ¶11 And Leah said, "Good fortune!" so she named him Gad. ¶12 Leah's maid Zilpah bore Jacob a second son. ¶13 And Leah said, "Happy am I! For the women will call me happy"; so she named him Asher. ¶14 In the days of wheat harvest Reuben went and found mandrakes in the field, and brought them to his mother Leah. Then Rachel said to Leah, "Please give me some of your son's mandrakes." ¶15 But she said to her, "Is it a small matter that you have taken away my husband? Would you take away my son's mandrakes also?" Rachel said, "Then he may lie with you tonight for your son's mandrakes." ¶16 When Jacob came from the field in the evening, Leah went out to meet him, and said, "You must come in to me; for I have hired you with my son's mandrakes." So he lay with her that night. ¶17 And God

heeded Leah, and she conceived and bore Jacob a fifth son. ¶18 Leah said, "God has given me my hire because I gave my maid to my husband"; so she named him Issachar. ¶19 And Leah conceived again, and she bore Jacob a sixth son. ¶20 Then Leah said, "God has endowed me with a good dowry; now my husband will honor me, because I have borne him six sons"; so she named him Zebulun. ¶21 Afterwards she bore a daughter, and named her Dinah. ¶22 Then God remembered Rachel, and God heeded her and opened her womb. ¶23 She conceived and bore a son, and said, "God has taken away my reproach"; ¶24 and she named him Joseph, saying, "May the LORD add to me another son!" ¶25 When Rachel had borne Joseph, Jacob said to Laban, "Send me away, that I may go to my own home and country. ¶26 Give me my wives and my children for whom I have served you, and let me go; for you know very well the service I have given you." ¶27 But Laban said to him, "If you will allow me to say so, I have learned by divination that the LORD has blessed me because of you; ¶28 name your wages, and I will give it." ¶29 Jacob said to him, "You yourself know how I have served you, and how your cattle have fared with me. ¶30 For you had little before I came, and it has increased abundantly; and the LORD has blessed you wherever I turned. But now when shall I provide for my own household also?" ¶31 He said, "What shall I give you?" Jacob said, "You shall not give me anything; if you will do this for me, I will again feed your flock and keep it: ¶32 let me pass through all your flock today, removing from it every speckled and spot-

ted sheep and every black lamb, and the spotted and speckled among the goats; and such shall be my wages. ¶33 So my honesty will answer for me later, when you come to look into my wages with you. Every one that is not speckled and spotted among the goats and black among the lambs, if found with me, shall be counted stolen." ¶34 Laban said, "Good! Let it be as you have said." ¶35 But that day Laban removed the male goats that were striped and spotted, and all the female goats that were speckled and spotted, every one that had white on it, and every lamb that was black, and put them in charge of his sons; ¶36 and he set a distance of three days' journey between himself and Jacob, while Jacob was pasturing the rest of Laban's flock. ¶37 Then Jacob took fresh rods of poplar and almond and plane, and peeled white streaks in them, exposing the white of the rods. ¶38 He set the rods that he had peeled in front of the flocks in the troughs, that is, the watering places, where the flocks came to drink. And since they bred when they came to drink, ¶39 the flocks bred in front of the rods, and so the flocks produced young that were striped, speckled, and spotted. ¶40 Jacob separated the lambs, and set the faces of the flocks toward the striped and the completely black animals in the flock of Laban; and he put his own droves apart, and did not put them with Laban's flock. ¶41 Whenever the stronger of the flock were breeding, Jacob laid the rods in the troughs before the eyes of the flock, that they might breed among the rods, ¶42 but for the feebler of the flock he did not lay them there; so the feebler were Laban's, and the stronger Jacob's. ¶43 Thus the man grew exceedingly rich, and had large flocks, and male and female slaves, and camels and donkeys.

31 ¶1 Now Jacob heard that the sons of Laban were saying, "Jacob has taken all that was our father's; he has gained all this wealth from what belonged to our father." ¶2 And Jacob saw that Laban did not regard him as favorably as he did before. ¶3 Then the LORD said to Jacob, "Return to the land of your ancestors and to your kindred, and I will be with you." ¶4 So Jacob sent and called Rachel and Leah into the field where his flock was, ¶5 and said to them, "I see that your father does not regard me as favorably as he did before. But the God of my father has been with me. ¶6 You know that I have served your father with all my strength; ¶7 yet your father has cheated me and changed my wages ten times, but God did not permit him to harm me. ¶8 If he said, 'The speckled shall be your wages,' then all the flock bore speckled; and if he said, 'The striped shall be your wages,' then all the flock bore striped. ¶9 Thus God has taken away the livestock of your father, and given them to me. ¶10 During the mating of the flock I once had a dream in which I looked up and saw that the male goats that leaped upon the flock were striped, speckled, and mottled. ¶11 Then the angel of God said to me in the dream, 'Jacob,' and I said, 'Here I am!' ¶12 And he said, 'Look up and see that all the goats that leap on the flock are striped, speckled, and mottled; for I have seen all that Laban is

doing to you. ¶13 I am the God of Bethel, where you anointed a pillar and made a vow to me. Now leave this land at once and return to the land of your birth.' " ¶14 Then Rachel and Leah answered him, "Is there any portion or inheritance left to us in our father's house? ¶15 Are we not regarded by him as foreigners? For he has sold us, and he has been using up the money given for us. ¶16 All the property that God has taken away from our father belongs to us and to our children; now then, do whatever God has said to you." ¶17 So Jacob arose, and set his children and his wives on camels; ¶18 and he drove away all his livestock, all the property that he had gained, the livestock in his possession that he had acquired in Paddan-aram, to go to his father Isaac in the land of Canaan. ¶19 Now Laban had gone to shear his sheep, and Rachel stole her father's household gods. ¶20 And Jacob deceived Laban the Aramean, in that he did not tell him that he intended to flee. ¶21 So he fled with all that he had; starting out he crossed the Euphrates, and set his face toward the hill country of Gilead. ¶22 On the third day Laban was told that Jacob had fled. ¶23 So he took his kinsfolk with him and pursued him for seven days until he caught up with him in the hill country of Gilead. ¶24 But God came to Laban the Aramean in a dream by night, and said to him, "Take heed that you say not a word to Jacob, either good or bad." ¶25 Laban overtook Jacob. Now Jacob had pitched his tent in the hill country, and Laban with his kinsfolk camped in the hill country of Gilead. ¶26 Laban said to Jacob, "What have you done? You have deceived me, and carried away my daughters like captives of the sword. ¶27 Why did you flee secretly and deceive me and not tell me? I would have sent you away with mirth and songs, with tambourine and lyre. ¶28 And why did you not permit me to kiss my sons and my daughters farewell? What you have done is foolish. ¶29 It is in my power to do you harm; but the God of your father spoke to me last night, saying, 'Take heed that you speak to Jacob neither good nor bad.' ¶30 Even though you had to go because you longed greatly for your father's house, why did you steal my gods?" ¶31 Jacob answered Laban, "Because I was afraid, for I thought that you would take your daughters from me by force. ¶32 But anyone with whom you find your gods shall not live. In the presence of our kinsfolk, point out what I have that is yours, and take it." Now Jacob did not know that Rachel had stolen the gods. ¶33 So Laban went into Jacob's tent, and into Leah's tent, and into the tent of the two maids, but he did not find them. And he went out of Leah's tent, and entered Rachel's. ¶34 Now Rachel had taken the household gods and put them in the camel's saddle, and sat on them. Laban felt all about in the tent, but did not find them. ¶35 And she said to her father, "Let not my lord be angry that I cannot rise before you, for the way of women is upon me." So he searched, but did not find the household gods. ¶36 Then Jacob became angry, and upbraided Laban. Jacob said to Laban, "What is my offense? What is my sin, that you have hotly pursued me? ¶37 Although you have felt about through all my goods, what have you found of all your household goods? Set it here before my kinsfolk and your kinsfolk, so that they may decide between us two. ¶38 These twenty years I have been with you; your ewes and your female goats have not miscarried, and I have not eaten the rams of your flocks. ¶39 That which was torn by wild beasts I did not bring to you; I bore the loss of it myself; of my hand you required it, whether stolen by day or stolen by night. ¶40 It was like this with me: by day the heat consumed me, and the cold by night, and my sleep fled from my eyes. ¶41 These twenty years I have been in your house; I served you fourteen years for your two daughters, and six years for your flock, and you have changed my wages ten times. ¶42 If the God of my father, the God of Abraham and the Fear of Isaac, had not been on my side, surely now you would have sent me away empty-handed. God saw my affliction and the labor of my hands, and rebuked you last night." ¶43 Then Laban answered and said to Jacob, "The daughters are my daughters, the children are my children, the flocks are my flocks, and all that you see is mine. But what can I do today about these daughters of mine, or about their children whom they have borne? ¶44 Come now, let us make a covenant, you and I; and let it be a witness between you and me." ¶45 So Jacob took a stone, and set it up as a pillar. ¶46 And Jacob said to his kinsfolk, "Gather stones," and they took stones, and made a heap; and they ate there by the heap. ¶47 Laban called it Jegarsahadutha: but Jacob called it Galeed. ¶48 Laban said, "This heap is a witness between you and me today." Therefore he called it Galeed, ¶49 and the pillar Mizpah, for he said, "The LORD watch between you and me, when we are absent one from the other. ¶50 If you ill-treat my daughters, or if you take wives in addition to my daughters, though no one else is with us, remember that God is witness between you and me." ¶51 Then Laban said to Jacob, "See this heap and see the pillar, which I have set between you and me. ¶52 This heap is a witness, and the pillar is a witness, that I will not pass beyond this heap to you, and you will not pass beyond this heap and this pillar to me, for harm. ¶53 May the God of Abraham and the God of Nahor"—the God of their father— "judge between us." So Jacob swore by the Fear of his father Isaac, ¶54 and Jacob offered a sacrifice on the height and called his kinsfolk to eat bread; and they ate bread and tarried all night in the hill country. ¶55 Early in the morning Laban rose up, and kissed his grandchildren and his daughters and blessed them; then he departed and returned home.

32 ¶1 Jacob went on his way and the angels of God met him; ¶2 and when Jacob saw them he said, "This is God's camp!" So he called that place Mahanaim. ¶3 Jacob sent messengers before him to his brother Esau in the land of Seir, the country of Edom, ¶4 instructing them, "Thus you shall say to my lord Esau: Thus says your servant Jacob, 'I have lived with Laban as an alien, and stayed until now; ¶5 and I have oxen, donkeys, flocks, male and female slaves; and I have sent to tell my lord, in order that I may find favor in your sight.'" ¶6 The messengers returned to Jacob, saying, "We

came to your brother Esau, and he is coming to meet you, and four hundred men are with him." ¶7 Then Jacob was greatly afraid and distressed; and he divided the people that were with him, and the flocks and herds and camels, into two companies, ¶8 thinking, "If Esau comes to the one company and destroys it, then the company that is left will escape." ¶9 And Jacob said, "O God of my father Abraham and God of my father Isaac, O LORD who said to me, 'Return to your country and to your kindred, and I will do you good,' ¶10 I am not worthy of the least of all the steadfast love and all the faithfulness that you have shown to your servant, for with only my staff I crossed this Jordan; and now I have become two companies. ¶11 Deliver me, please, from the hand of my brother, from the hand of Esau, for I am afraid of him; he may come and kill us all, the mothers with the children. ¶12 Yet you have said, 'I will surely do you good, and make your offspring as the sand of the sea, which cannot be counted because of their number.'" ¶13 So he spent that night there, and from what he had with him he took a present for his brother Esau, ¶14 two hundred female goats and twenty male goats, two hundred ewes and twenty rams, ¶15 thirty milch camels and their colts, forty cows and ten bulls, twenty female donkeys and ten male donkeys. ¶16 These he delivered into the hand of his servants, every drove by itself, and said to his servants, "Pass on ahead of me, and put a space between drove and drove." ¶17 He instructed the foremost, "When Esau my brother meets you, and asks you, 'To whom do you belong? Where are you going? And whose are these ahead of you?' ¶18 then you shall say, 'They belong to your servant Jacob; they are a present sent to my lord Esau; and moreover he is behind us.' " ¶19 He likewise instructed the second and the third and all who followed the droves, "You shall say the same thing to Esau when you meet him, ¶20 and you shall say, 'Moreover your servant Jacob is behind us.' " For he thought, "I may appease him with the present that goes ahead of me, and afterwards I shall see his face; perhaps he will accept me." ¶21 So the present passed on ahead of him; and he himself spent that night in the camp. ¶22 The same night he got up and took his two wives, his two maids, and his eleven children, and crossed the ford of the Jabbok. ¶23 He took them and sent them across the stream, and likewise everything that he had. ¶24 Jacob was left alone; and a man wrestled with him until daybreak. ¶25 When the man saw that he did not prevail against Jacob, he struck him on the hip socket; and Jacob's hip was put out of joint as he wrestled with him. ¶26 Then he said, "Let me go, for the day is breaking." But Jacob said, "I will not let you go, unless you bless me." ¶27 So he said to him, "What is your name?" And he said, "Jacob." ¶28 Then the man said, "You shall no longer be called Jacob, but Israel, for you have striven with God and with humans, and have prevailed." ¶29 Then Jacob asked him, "Please tell me your name." But he said, "Why is it that you ask my name?" And there he blessed him. ¶30 So Jacob called the place Peniel, saying, "For I have seen God face to face, and yet my life is preserved." ¶31 The sun rose upon him as he passed Peniel, limping because of his hip. ¶32 Therefore to this day the Israelites do not eat the thigh muscle that is on the hip socket, because he struck Jacob on the hip socket at the thigh muscle.

33 ¶1 Now Jacob looked up and saw Esau coming, and four hundred men with him. So he divided the children among Leah and Rachel and the two maids. ¶2 He put the maids with their children in front, then Leah with her children, and Rachel and Joseph last of all. ¶3 He himself went on ahead of them, bowing himself to the ground seven times, until he came near his brother. ¶4 But Esau ran to meet him, and embraced him, and fell on his neck and kissed him, and they wept. ¶5 When Esau looked up and saw the women and children, he said, "Who are these with you?" Jacob said, "The children whom God has graciously given your servant." ¶6 Then the maids drew near, they and their children, and bowed down; ¶7 Leah likewise and her children drew near and bowed down; and finally Joseph and Rachel drew near, and they bowed down. ¶8 Esau said, "What do you mean by all this company that I met?" Jacob answered, "To find favor with my lord." ¶9 But Esau said, "I have enough, my brother; keep what you have for yourself." ¶10 Jacob said, "No, please; if I find favor with you, then accept my present from my hand; for truly to see your face is like seeing the face of God—since you have received me with such favor. ¶11 Please accept my gift that is brought to you, because God has dealt graciously with me

and because I have everything I want." So he urged him, and he took it. ¶12 Then Esau said, "Let us journey on our way, and I will go alongside you." ¶13 But Jacob said to him, "My lord knows that the children are frail and that the flocks and herds, which are nursing, are a care to me, and if they are overdriven for one day, all the flocks will die. ¶14 Let my lord pass on ahead of his servant, and I will lead on slowly, according to the pace of the cattle that are before me and according to the pace of the children, until I come to my lord in Seir." ¶15 So Esau said, "Let me leave with you some of the people who are with me." But he said, "Why should my lord be so kind to me?" ¶16 So Esau returned that day on his way to Seir. ¶17 But Jacob journeyed to Succoth, and built himself a house, and made booths for his cattle; therefore the place is called Succoth. ¶18 Jacob came safely to the city of Shechem, which is in the land of Canaan, on his way from Paddan-aram; and he camped before the city. ¶19 And from the sons of Hamor, Shechem's father, he bought for one hundred pieces of money the plot of land on which he had pitched his tent. ¶20 There he erected an altar and called it El-Elohe-Israel.

34 ¶1 Now Dinah the daughter of Leah, whom she had borne to Jacob, went out to visit the women of the region. ¶2 When Shechem son of Hamor the Hivite, prince of the region, saw her, he seized her and lay with her by force. ¶3 And his soul was drawn to Dinah daughter of Jacob; he loved the girl, and spoke tenderly to her. ¶4 So Shechem spoke to his father Hamor, saying, "Get me this girl to be my wife." ¶5 Now Jacob heard that Shechem had defiled his daughter Dinah; but his sons were with his cattle in the field, so Jacob held his peace until they came. ¶6 And Hamor the father of Shechem went out to Jacob to speak with him, ¶7 just as the sons of Jacob came in from the field. When they heard of it, the men were indignant and very angry, because he had committed an outrage in Israel by lying with Jacob's daughter, for such a thing ought not to be done. ¶8 But Hamor spoke with them, saying, "The heart of my son Shechem longs for your daughter; please give her to him in marriage. ¶9 Make marriages with us; give your daughters to us, and take our daughters for yourselves. ¶10 You shall live with us; and the land shall be open to you; live and trade in it, and get property in it." ¶11 Shechem also said to her father and to her brothers, "Let me find favor with you, and whatever you say to me I will give. ¶12 Put the marriage present and gift as high as you like, and I will give whatever you ask me; only give me the girl to be my wife." ¶13 The sons of Jacob answered Shechem and his father Hamor deceitfully, because he had defiled their sister Dinah. ¶14 They said to them, "We cannot do this thing, to give our sister to one who is uncircumcised, for that would be a disgrace to us. ¶15 Only on this condition will we consent to you: that you will become as we are and every male among you be circumcised. ¶16 Then we will give our daughters to you, and we will take your daughters for ourselves, and we will live among you

and become one people. ¶17 But if you will not listen to us and be circumcised, then we will take our daughter and be gone." ¶18 Their words pleased Hamor and Hamor's son Shechem. ¶19 And the young man did not delay to do the thing, because he was delighted with Jacob's daughter. Now he was the most honored of all his family. ¶20 So Hamor and his son Shechem came to the gate of their city and spoke to the men of their city, saying, ¶21 "These people are friendly with us; let them live in the land and trade in it, for the land is large enough for them; let us take their daughters in marriage, and let us give them our daughters. ¶22 Only on this condition will they agree to live among us, to become one people: that every male among us be circumcised as they are circumcised. ¶23 Will not their livestock, their property, and all their animals be ours? Only let us agree with them, and they will live among us." ¶24 And all who went out of the city gate heeded Hamor and his son Shechem; and every male was circumcised, all who went out of the gate of his city. ¶25 On the third day, when they were still in pain, two of the sons of Jacob, Simeon and Levi, Dinah's brothers, took their swords and came against the city unawares, and killed all the males. ¶26 They killed Hamor and his son Shechem with the sword, and took Dinah out of Shechem's house, and went away. ¶27 And the other sons of Jacob came upon the slain, and plundered the city, because their sister had been defiled. ¶28 They took their flocks and their herds, their donkeys, and whatever was in the city and in the field. ¶29 All their wealth, all their little ones and their wives, all that was in the

houses, they captured and made their prey. ¶30 Then Jacob said to Simeon and Levi, "You have brought trouble on me by making me odious to the inhabitants of the land, the Canaanites and the Perizzites; my numbers are few, and if they gather themselves against me and attack me, I shall be destroyed, both I and my household." ¶31 But they said, "Should our sister be treated like a whore?"

35 ¶1 God said to Jacob, "Arise, go up to Bethel, and settle there. Make an altar there to the God who appeared to you when you fled from your brother Esau." ¶2 So Jacob said to his household and to all who were with him, "Put away the foreign gods that are among you, and purify yourselves, and change your clothes; ¶3 then come, let us go up to Bethel, that I may make an altar there to the God who answered me in the day of my distress and has been with me wherever I have gone." ¶4 So they gave to Jacob all the foreign gods that they had, and the rings that were in their ears; and Jacob hid them under the oak that was near Shechem. ¶5 As they journeyed, a terror from God fell upon the cities all around them, so that no one pursued them. ¶6 Jacob came to Luz (that is, Bethel), which is in the land of Canaan, he and all the people who were with him, ¶7 and there he built an altar and called the place El-bethel, because it was there that God had revealed himself to him when he fled from his brother. ¶8 And Deborah, Rebekah's nurse, died, and she was buried under an oak below Bethel. So it was called Allon-

bacuth. ¶9 God appeared to Jacob again when he came from Paddan-aram, and he blessed him. ¶10 God said to him, "Your name is Jacob; no longer shall you be called Jacob, but Israel shall be your name." So he was called Israel. ¶11 God said to him, "I am God Almighty: be fruitful and multiply, a nation and a company of nations shall come from you, and kings shall spring from you. ¶12 The land that I gave to Abraham and Isaac I will give to you, and I will give the land to your offspring after you." ¶13 Then God went up from him at the place where he had spoken with him. ¶14 Jacob set up a pillar in the place where he had spoken with him, a pillar of stone; and he poured out a drink offering on it, and poured oil on it. ¶15 So Jacob called the place where God had spoken with him Bethel. ¶16 Then they journeyed from Bethel; and when they were still some distance from Ephrath, Rachel was in childbirth, and she had hard labor. ¶17 When she was in her hard labor, the midwife said to her, "Do not be afraid; for now you will have another son." ¶18 As her soul was departing (for she died), she named him Ben-oni; but his father called him Benjamin. ¶19 So Rachel died, and she was buried on the way to Ephrath (that is, Bethlehem), ¶20 and Jacob set up a pillar at her grave; it is the pillar of Rachel's tomb, which is there to this day. ¶21 Israel journeyed on, and pitched his tent beyond the tower of Eder. ¶22 While Israel lived in that land, Reuben went and lay with Bilhah his father's concubine; and Israel heard of it. Now the sons of Jacob were twelve. ¶23 The sons of Leah: Reuben (Jacob's firstborn), Simeon, Levi, Judah, Issachar, and

Zebulun. ¶24 The sons of Rachel: Joseph and Benjamin. ¶25 The sons of Bilhah, Rachel's maid: Dan and Naphtali. ¶26 The sons of Zilpah, Leah's maid: Gad and Asher. These were the sons of Jacob who were born to him in Paddan-aram. ¶27 Jacob came to his father Isaac at Mamre, or Kiriath-arba (that is, Hebron), where Abraham and Isaac had resided as aliens. ¶28 Now the days of Isaac were one hundred eighty years. ¶29 And Isaac breathed his last; he died and was gathered to his people, old and full of days; and his sons Esau and Jacob buried him.

36 ¶1 These are the descendants of Esau (that is, Edom). ¶2 Esau took his wives from the Canaanites: Adah daughter of Elon the Hittite, Oholibamah daughter of Anah son of Zibeon the Hivite, ¶3 and Basemath, Ishmael's daughter, sister of Nebaioth. ¶4 Adah bore Eliphaz to Esau; Basemath bore Reuel; ¶5 and Oholibamah bore Jeush, Jalam, and Korah. These are the sons of Esau who were born to him in the land of Canaan. ¶6 Then Esau took his wives, his sons, his daughters, and all the members of his household, his cattle, all his livestock, and all the property he had acquired in the land of Canaan; and he moved to a land some distance from his brother Jacob. ¶7 For their possessions were too great for them to live together; the land where they were staying could not support them because of their livestock. ¶8 So Esau settled in the hill country of Seir; Esau is Edom. ¶9 These are the descendants of Esau, ancestor of the Edomites, in the hill

country of Seir. ¶10 These are the names of Esau's sons: Eliphaz son of Adah the wife of Esau; Reuel, the son of Esau's wife Basemath. ¶11 The sons of Eliphaz were Teman, Omar, Zepho, Gatam, and Kenaz. ¶12 (Timna was a concubine of Eliphaz, Esau's son; she bore Amalek to Eliphaz.) These were the sons of Adah, Esau's wife. ¶13 These were the sons of Reuel: Nahath, Zerah, Shammah, and Mizzah. These were the sons of Esau's wife, Basemath. ¶14 These were the sons of Esau's wife Oholibamah, daughter of Anah son of Zibeon: she bore to Esau Jeush, Jalam, and Korah. ¶15 These are the clans of the sons of Esau. The sons of Eliphaz the first-born of Esau: the clans Teman, Omar, Zepho, Kenaz, ¶16 Korah, Gatam, and Amalek; these are the clans of Eliphaz in the land of Edom; they are the sons of Adah. ¶17 These are the sons of Esau's son Reuel: the clans Nahath, Zerah, Shammah, and Mizzah; these are the clans of Reuel in the land of Edom; they are the sons of Esau's wife Basemath. ¶18 These are the sons of Esau's wife Oholibamah: the clans Jeush, Jalam, and Korah; these are the clans born of Esau's wife Oholibamah, the daughter of Anah. ¶19 These are the sons of Esau (that is, Edom), and these are their clans. ¶20 These are the sons of Seir the Horite, the inhabitants of the land: Lotan, Shobal, Zibeon, Anah, ¶21 Dishon, Ezer, and Dishan; these are the clans of the Horites, the sons of Seir in the land of Edom. ¶22 The sons of Lotan were Hori and Heman; and Lotan's sister was Timna. ¶23 These are the sons of Shobal: Alvan, Manahath, Ebal, Shepho, and Onam. ¶24 These are the sons of Zibeon: Aiah and Anah; he is the Anah who found the springs in the wilderness, as he pastured the donkeys of his father Zibeon. ¶25 These are the children of Anah: Dishon and Oholibamah daughter of Anah. ¶26 These are the sons of Dishon: Hemdan, Eshban, Ithran, and Cheran. ¶27 These are the sons of Ezer: Bilhan, Zaavan, and Akan. ¶28 These are the sons of Dishan: Uz and Aran. ¶29 These are the clans of the Horites, the clans Lotan, Shobal, Zibeon, Anah, ¶30 Dishon, Ezer, and Dishan; these are the clans of the Horites, clan by clan in the land of Seir. ¶31 These are the kings who reigned in the land of Edom, before any king reigned over the Israelites. ¶32 Bela son of Beor reigned in Edom, the name of his city being Dinhabah. ¶33 Bela died, and Jobab son of Zerah of Bozrah succeeded him as king. ¶34 Jobab died, and Husham of the land of the Temanites succeeded him as king. ¶35 Husham died, and Hadad son of Bedad, who defeated Midian in the country of Moab, succeeded him as king, the name of his city being Avith. ¶36 Hadad died, and Samlah of Masrekah succeeded him as king. ¶37 Samlah died, and Shaul of Rehoboth on the Euphrates succeeded him as king. ¶38 Shaul died, and Baal-hanan son of Achbor succeeded him as king. ¶39 Baal-hanan son of Achbor died, and Hadar succeeded him as king, the name of his city being Pau; his wife's name was Mehetabel, the daughter of Matred, daughter of Mezahab. ¶40 These are the names of the clans of Esau, according to their families and their localities by their names: the clans Timna, Alvah, Jetheth, ¶41 Oholibamah, Elah, Pinon, ¶42 Kenaz, Teman, Mibzar,

¶43 Magdiel, and Iram; these are the clans of Edom (that is, Esau, the father of Edom), according to their settlements in the land that they held.

37 ¶1 Jacob settled in the land where his father had lived as an alien, the land of Canaan. ¶2 This is the story of the family of Jacob. Joseph, being seventeen years old, was shepherding the flock with his brothers; he was a helper to the sons of Bilhah and Zilpah, his father's wives; and Joseph brought a bad report of them to their father. ¶3 Now Israel loved Joseph more than any other of his children, because he was the son of his old age; and he had made him a long robe with sleeves. ¶4 But when his brothers saw that their father loved him more than all his brothers, they hated him, and could not speak peaceably to him. ¶5 Once Joseph had a dream, and when he told it to his brothers, they hated him even more. ¶6 He said to them, "Listen to this dream that I dreamed. ¶7 There we were, binding sheaves in the field. Suddenly my sheaf rose and stood upright; then your sheaves gathered around it, and bowed down to my sheaf." ¶8 His brothers said to him, "Are you indeed to reign over us? Are you indeed to have dominion over us?" So they hated him even more because of his dreams and his words. ¶9 He had another dream, and told it to his brothers, saying, "Look, I have had another dream: the sun, the moon, and eleven stars were bowing down to me." ¶10 But when he told it to his father and to his brothers, his father rebuked him, and said to him, "What kind of dream is this that

you have had? Shall we indeed come, I and your mother and your brothers, and bow to the ground before you?" ¶11 So his brothers were jealous of him, but his father kept the matter in mind. ¶12 Now his brothers went to pasture their father's flock near Shechem. ¶13 And Israel said to Joseph, "Are not your brothers pasturing the flock at Shechem? Come, I will send you to them." He answered, "Here I am." ¶14 So he said to him. "Go now, see if it is well with your brothers and with the flock; and bring word back to me." So he sent him from the valley of Hebron. He came to Shechem, ¶15 and a man found him wandering in the fields; the man asked him, "What are you seeking?" ¶16 "I am seeking my brothers," he said; "tell me, please, where they are pasturing the flock." ¶17 The man said, "They have gone away, for I heard them say, 'Let us go to Dothan.' " So Joseph went after his brothers, and found them at Dothan. ¶18 They saw him from a distance, and before he came near to them, they conspired to kill him. ¶19 They said to one another, "Here comes this dreamer. ¶20 Come now, let us kill him and throw him into one of the pits; then we shall say that a wild animal has devoured him, and we shall see what will become of his dreams." ¶21 But when Reuben heard it, he delivered him out of their hands, saying, "Let us not take his life." ¶22 Reuben said to them, "Shed no blood; throw him into this pit here in the wilderness, but lay no hand on him"—that he might rescue him out of their hand and restore him to his father. ¶23 So when Joseph came to his brothers, they stripped him of his robe, the long robe with sleeves that he wore;

¶24 and they took him and threw him into a pit. The pit was empty; there was no water in it. ¶25 Then they sat down to eat; and looking up they saw a caravan of Ishmaelites coming from Gilead, with their camels carrying gum, balm, and resin, on their way to carry it down to Egypt. ¶26 Then Judah said to his brothers, "What profit is it if we kill our brother and conceal his blood? ¶27 Come, let us sell him to the Ishmaelites, and not lay our hands on him, for he is our brother, our own flesh." And his brothers agreed. ¶28 When some Midianite traders passed by, they drew Joseph up, lifting him out of the pit, and sold him to the Ishmaelites for twenty pieces of silver. And they took Joseph to Egypt. ¶29 When Reuben returned to the pit and saw that Joseph was not in the pit, he tore his clothes. ¶30 He returned to his brothers, and said, "The boy is gone; and I, where can I turn?" ¶31 Then they took Joseph's robe, slaughtered a goat, and dipped the robe in the blood. ¶32 They had the long robe with sleeves taken to their father, and they said, "This we have found; see now whether it is your son's robe or not." ¶33 He recognized it, and said, "It is my son's robe! A wild animal has devoured him; Joseph is without doubt torn to pieces." ¶34 Then Jacob tore his garments, and put sackcloth on his loins, and mourned for his son many days. ¶35 All his sons and all his daughters sought to comfort him; but he refused to be comforted, and said, "No, I shall go down to Sheol to my son, mourning." Thus his father bewailed him. ¶36 Meanwhile the Midianites had sold him in Egypt to Potiphar, one of Pharaoh's officials, the captain of the guard.

38 ¶1 It happened at that time that Judah went down from his brothers and settled near a certain Adullamite whose name was Hirah. ¶2 There Judah saw the daughter of a certain Canaanite whose name was Shua; he married her and went in to her. ¶3 She conceived and bore a son; and he named him Er. ¶4 Again she conceived and bore a son whom she named Onan. ¶5 Yet again she bore a son; and she named him Shelah. She was in Chezib when she bore him. ¶6 Judah took a wife for Er his firstborn; her name was Tamar. ¶7 But Er, Judah's firstborn, was wicked in the sight of the LORD, and the LORD put him to death. ¶8 Then Judah said to Onan, "Go in to your brother's wife and perform the duty of a brother-in-law to her; raise up offspring for your brother." ¶9 But since Onan knew that the offspring would not be his, spilled his semen on the ground whenever he went in to his brother's wife, so that he would not give offspring to his brother. ¶10 What he did was displeasing in the sight of the LORD, and he put him to death also. ¶11 Then Judah said to his daughter-in-law Tamar, "Remain a widow in your father's house until my son Shelah grows up"—for he feared that he too would die, like his brothers. So Tamar went to live in her father's house. ¶12 In course of time the wife of Judah, Shua's daughter, died; when Judah's time of mourning was over, he went up to Timnah to his sheepshearers, he and his friend Hirah the Adulamite. ¶13 When Tamar was told, "Your father-in-law is going up to Timnah to shear his sheep," ¶14 she put off her widow's garments, put on a veil, wrapped herself up, and sat down

at the entrance to Enaim, which is on the road to Timnah. She saw that Shelah was grown up, yet she had not been given to him in marriage. ¶15 When Judah saw her, he thought her to be a prostitute, for she had covered her face. ¶16 He went over to her at the roadside, and said, "Come, let me come in to you," for he did not know that she was his daughter-in-law. She said, "What will you give me, that you may come in to me?" ¶17 He answered, "I will send you a kid from the flock." And she said, "Only if you give me a pledge, until you send it." ¶18 He said, "What pledge shall I give you?" She replied, "Your signet and your cord, and the staff that is in your hand." So he gave them to her, and went in to her, and she conceived by him. ¶19 Then she got up and went away, and taking off her veil she put on the garments of her widowhood. ¶20 When Judah sent the kid by his friend the Adullamite, to recover the pledge from the woman, he could not find her. ¶21 He asked the townspeople, "Where is the temple prostitute who was at Enaim by the wayside?" But they said, "No prostitute has been here." ¶22 So he returned to Judah, and said, "I have not found her; moreover the townspeople said, 'No prostitute has been here.'" ¶23 Judah replied, "Let her keep the things as her own, otherwise we will be laughed at; you see, I sent this kid, and you could not find her." ¶24 About three months later Judah was told, "Your daughter-in-law Tamar has played the whore; moreover she is pregnant as a result of whoredom." And Judah said, "Bring her out, and let her be burned." ¶25 As she was being brought out, she sent word to her father-in-law, "It was the owner of these who made me pregnant." And she said, "Take note, please, whose these are, the signet and the cord and the staff." ¶26 Then Judah acknowledged them and said, "She is more in the right than I, since I did not give her to my son Shelah." And he did not lie with her again. ¶27 When the time of her delivery came, there were twins in her womb. ¶28 While she was in labor, one put out a hand; and the midwife took and bound on his hand a crimson thread, saying, "This one came out first." ¶29 But just then he drew back his hand, and out came his brother; and she said, "What a breach you have made for yourself!" Therefore he was named Perez. ¶30 Afterward his brother came out with the crimson thread on his hand; and he was named Zerah.

39 ¶1 Now Joseph was taken down to Egypt, and Potiphar, an officer of Pharaoh, the captain of the guard, an Egyptian, bought him from the Ishmaelites who had brought him down there. ¶2 The LORD was with Joseph, and he became a successful man; he was in the house of his Egyptian master. ¶3 His master saw that the LORD was with him, and that the LORD caused all that he did to prosper in his hands. ¶4 So Joseph found favor in his sight and attended him; he made him overseer of his house and put him in charge of all that he had. ¶5 From the time that he made him overseer in his house and over all that he had, the LORD blessed the Egyptian's house for Joseph's sake; the blessing of the LORD was on all that he had, in house and field. ¶6 So he

left all that he had in Joseph's charge; and, with him there, he had no concern for anything but the food that he ate. Now Joseph was handsome and good-looking. ¶7 And after a time his master's wife cast her eyes on Joseph and said, "Lie with me." ¶8 But he refused and said to his master's wife, "Look, with me here, my master has no concern about anything in the house, and he has put everything that he has in my hand. ¶9 He is not greater in this house than I am, nor has he kept back anything from me except yourself, because you are his wife. How then could I do this great wickedness, and sin against God?" ¶10 And although she spoke to Joseph day after day, he would not consent to lie beside her or to be with her. ¶11 One day, however, when he went into the house to do his work, and while no one else was in the house, ¶12 she caught hold of his garment, saying, "Lie with me!" But he left his garment in her hand, and fled and ran outside. ¶13 When she saw that he had left his garment in her hand and had fled outside, ¶14 she called out to the members of her household and said to them, "See, my husband has brought among us a Hebrew to insult us! He came in to me to lie with me, and I cried out with a loud voice; ¶15 and when he heard me raise my voice and cry out, he left his garment beside me, and fled outside." ¶16 Then she kept his garment by her until his master came home, ¶17 and she told him the same story, saying, "The Hebrew servant, whom you have brought among us, came in to me to insult me; ¶18 but as soon as I raised my voice and cried out, he left his garment beside me, and fled outside." ¶19 When his mas-

ter heard the words that his wife spoke t him, saying, "This is the way your servar treated me," he became enraged. ¶2 And Joseph's master took him and put hi into the prison, the place where the king prisoners were confined; he remained the in prison. ¶21 But the LORD was wit Joseph and showed him steadfast love; h gave him favor in the sight of the chi jailer. ¶22 The chief jailer committed Joseph's care all the prisoners who were the prison, and whatever was done ther he was the one who did it. ¶23 The chi jailer paid no heed to anything that was Joseph's care, because the LORD was wi him; and whatever he did, the LORD made prosper.

40 ¶1 Some time after this, the cu bearer of the king of Egypt a his baker offended their lord t king of Egypt. ¶2 Pharaoh was ang with his two officers, the chief cupbear and the chief baker, ¶3 and he put them custody in the house of the captain the guard, in the prison where Joseph w confined. ¶4 The captain of the gua charged Joseph with them, and he wait on them; and they continued for sor time in custody. ¶5 One night they bo dreamed—the cupbearer and the baker the king of Egypt, who were confined the prison—each his own dream, and ea dream with its own meaning. ¶6 Wh Joseph came to them in the morning, saw that they were troubled. ¶7 So asked Pharaoh's officers, who were w him in custody in his master's house, "W are your faces downcast today?" ¶8 Th

said to him, "We have had dreams, and there is no one to interpret them." And Joseph said to them, "Do not interpretations belong to God? Please tell them to me." ¶9 So the chief cupbearer told his dream to Joseph, and said to him, "In my dream there was a vine before me, ¶10 and on the vine there were three branches. As soon as it budded, its blossoms came out and the clusters ripened into grapes. ¶11 Pharaoh's cup was in my hand; and I took the grapes and pressed them into Pharaoh's cup, and placed the cup in Pharaoh's hand." ¶12 Then Joseph said to him, "This is its interpretation: the three branches are three days; ¶13 within three days Pharaoh will lift up your head and restore you to your office; and you shall place Pharaoh's cup in his hand, just as you used to do when you were his cupbearer. ¶14 But remember me when it is well with you; please do me the kindness to make mention of me to Pharaoh, and so get me out of this place. ¶15 For in fact I was stolen out of the land of the Hebrews; and here also I have done nothing that they should have put me into the dungeon." ¶16 When the chief baker saw that the interpretation was favorable, he said to Joseph, "I also had a dream: there were three cake baskets on my head, ¶17 and in the uppermost basket there were all sorts of baked food for Pharaoh, but the birds were eating it out of the basket on my head." ¶18 And Joseph answered, "This is its interpretation: the three baskets are three days; ¶19 within three days Pharaoh will lift up your head—from you!—and hang you on a pole; and the birds will eat the flesh from you." ¶20 On the third day, which was Pharaoh's birthday, he made a feast for all his servants, and lifted up the head of the chief cupbearer and the head of the chief baker among his servants. ¶21 He restored the chief cupbearer to his cupbearing, and he placed the cup in Pharaoh's hand; ¶22 but the chief baker he hanged, just as Joseph had interpreted to them. ¶23 Yet the chief cupbearer did not remember Joseph, but forgot him.

41 ¶1 After two whole years, Pharaoh dreamed that he was standing by the Nile, ¶2 and there came up out of the Nile seven sleek and fat cows, and they grazed in the reed grass. ¶3 Then seven other cows, ugly and thin, came up out of the Nile after them, and stood by the other cows on the bank of the Nile. ¶4 The ugly and thin cows ate up the seven sleek and fat cows. And Pharaoh awoke. ¶5 Then he fell asleep and dreamed a second time; seven ears of grain, plump and good, were growing on one stalk. ¶6 Then seven ears, thin and blighted by the east wind, sprouted after them. ¶7 The thin ears swallowed up the seven plump and full ears. Pharaoh awoke, and it was a dream. ¶8 In the morning his spirit was troubled; so he sent and called for all the magicians of Egypt and all its wise men. Pharaoh told them his dreams, but there was no one who could interpret them to Pharaoh. ¶9 Then the chief cupbearer said to Pharaoh, "I remember my faults today. ¶10 Once Pharaoh was angry with his servants, and put me and the chief baker in custody in the house of the captain of the guard. ¶11 We dreamed on the same night, he and I, each

having a dream with its own meaning. ¶12 A young Hebrew was there with us, a servant of the captain of the guard. When we told him, he interpreted our dreams to us, giving an interpretation to each according to his dream. ¶13 As he interpreted to us, so it turned out; I was restored to my office, and the baker was hanged." ¶14 Then Pharaoh sent for Joseph, and he was hurriedly brought out of the dungeon. When he had shaved himself and changed his clothes, he came in before Pharaoh. ¶15 And Pharaoh said to Joseph, "I have had a dream, and there is no one who can interpret it. I have heard it said of you that when you hear a dream you can interpret it." ¶16 Joseph answered Pharaoh, "It is not I; God will give Pharaoh a favorable answer." ¶17 Then Pharaoh said to Joseph, "In my dream I was standing on the banks of the Nile; ¶18 and seven cows, fat and sleek, came up out of the Nile and fed in the reed grass. ¶19 Then seven other cows came up after them, poor, very ugly, and thin. Never had I seen such ugly ones in all the land of Egypt. ¶20 The thin and ugly cows ate up the first seven fat cows, ¶21 but when they had eaten them no one would have known that they had done so, for they were still as ugly as before. Then I awoke. ¶22 I fell asleep a second time and I saw in my dream seven ears of grain, full and good, growing on one stalk, ¶23 and seven ears, withered, thin, and blighted by the east wind, sprouting after them; ¶24 and the thin ears swallowed up the seven good ears. But when I told it to the magicians, there was no one who could explain it to me." ¶25 Then Joseph said to Pharaoh, "Pharaoh's dreams are one and

the same; God has revealed to Pharaoh what he is about to do. ¶26 The seven good cows are seven years, and the seven good ears are seven years; the dreams are one. ¶27 The seven lean and ugly cows that came up after them are seven years, as are the seven empty ears blighted by the east wind. They are seven years of famine. ¶28 It is as I told Pharaoh; God has shown to Pharaoh what he is about to do. ¶29 There will come seven years of great plenty throughout all the land of Egypt. ¶30 After them there will arise seven years of famine, and all the plenty will be forgotten in the land of Egypt; the famine will consume the land. ¶31 The plenty will no longer be known in the land because of the famine that will follow, for it will be very grievous. ¶32 And the doubling of Pharaoh's dream means that the thing is fixed by God, and God will shortly bring it about. ¶33 Now therefore let Pharaoh select a man who is discerning and wise, and set him over the land of Egypt. ¶34 Let Pharaoh proceed to appoint overseers over the land, and take one-fifth of the produce of the land of Egypt during the seven plenteous years. ¶35 Let them gather all the food of these good years that are coming, and lay up grain under the authority of Pharaoh for food in the cities, and let them keep it. ¶36 That food shall be a reserve for the land against the seven years of famine that are to befall the land of Egypt, so that the land may not perish through the famine." ¶37 The proposal pleased Pharaoh and all his servants. ¶38 Pharaoh said to his servants, "Can we find anyone else like this—one in whom is the spirit of God?" ¶39 So Pharaoh said to Joseph,

"Since God has shown you all this, there is no one so discerning and wise as you. ¶40 You shall be over my house, and all my people shall order themselves as you command; only with regard to the throne will I be greater than you." ¶41 And Pharaoh said to Joseph, "See, I have set you over all the land of Egypt." ¶42 Removing his signet ring from his hand, Pharaoh put it on Joseph's hand; he arrayed him in garments of fine linen, and put a gold chain around his neck. ¶43 He had him ride in the chariot of his second-in-command; and they cried out in front of him, "Bow the knee!" Thus he set him over all the land of Egypt. ¶44 Moreover Pharaoh said to Joseph, "I am Pharaoh, and without your consent no one shall lift up hand or foot in all the land of Egypt." ¶45 Pharaoh gave Joseph the name Zaphenathpaneah; and he gave him Asenath daughter of Potiphera, priest of On, as his wife. Thus Joseph gained authority over the land of Egypt. ¶46 Joseph was thirty years old when he entered the service of Pharaoh king of Egypt. And Joseph went out from the presence of Pharaoh, and went through all the land of Egypt. ¶47 During the seven plenteous years the earth produced abundantly. ¶48 He gathered up all the food of the seven years when there was plenty in the land of Egypt, and stored up food in the cities; he stored up in every city the food from the fields around it. ¶49 So Joseph stored up grain in such abundance—like the sand of the sea—that he stopped measuring it; it was beyond measure. ¶50 Before the years of famine came, Joseph had two sons, whom Asenath daughter of Potiphera, priest of On, bore to him. ¶51 Joseph named the firstborn Manasseh, "For," he said, "God has made me forget all my hardship and all my father's house." ¶52 The second he named Ephraim, "For God has made me fruitful in the land of my misfortunes." ¶53 The seven years of plenty that prevailed in the land of Egypt came to an end; ¶54 and the seven years of famine began to come, just as Joseph had said. There was famine in every country, but throughout the land of Egypt there was bread. ¶55 When all the land of Egypt was famished, the people cried to Pharaoh for bread. Pharaoh said to all the Egyptians, "Go to Joseph; what he says to you, do." ¶56 And since the famine had spread over all the land, Joseph opened all the storehouses, and sold to the Egyptians, for the famine was severe in the land of Egypt. ¶57 Moreover, all the world came to Joseph in Egypt to buy grain, because the famine became severe throughout the world.

42 ¶1 When Jacob learned that there was grain in Egypt, he said to his sons, "Why do you keep looking at one another? ¶2 I have heard," he said, "that there is grain in Egypt; go down and buy grain for us there, that we may live and not die." ¶3 So ten of Joseph's brothers went down to buy grain in Egypt. ¶4 But Jacob did not send Joseph's brother Benjamin with his brothers, for he feared that harm might come to him. ¶5 Thus the sons of Israel were among the other people who came to buy grain, for the famine had reached the land of Canaan. ¶6 Now Joseph was governor over the land; it was he who sold to all the

people of the land. And Joseph's brothers came and bowed themselves before him with their faces to the ground. ¶7 When Joseph saw his brothers, he recognized them, but he treated them like strangers and spoke harshly to them. "Where do you come from?" he said. They said, "From the land of Canaan, to buy food." ¶8 Although Joseph had recognized his brothers, they did not recognize him. ¶9 Joseph also remembered the dreams that he had dreamed about them. He said to them, "You are spies; you have come to see the nakedness of the land!" ¶10 They said to him, "No, my lord; your servants have come to buy food. ¶11 We are all sons of one man; we are honest men; your servants have never been spies." ¶12 But he said to them, "No, you have come to see the nakedness of the land!" ¶13 They said, "We, your servants, are twelve brothers, the sons of a certain man in the land of Canaan; the youngest, however, is now with our father, and one is no more." ¶14 But Joseph said to them, "It is just as I have said to you; you are spies! ¶15 Here is how you shall be tested: as Pharaoh lives, you shall not leave this place unless your youngest brother comes here! ¶16 Let one of you go and bring your brother, while the rest of you remain in prison, in order that your words may be tested, whether there is truth in you; or else, as Pharaoh lives, surely you are spies." ¶17 And he put them all together in prison for three days. ¶18 On the third day Joseph said to them, "Do this and you will live, for I fear God: ¶19 if you are honest men, let one of your brothers stay here where you are imprisoned. The rest of you shall go and carry grain for the famine of your households, ¶20 and bring your youngest brother to me. Thus your words will be verified, and you shall not die." And they agreed to do so. ¶21 They said to one another, "Alas, we are paying the penalty for what we did to our brother; we saw his anguish when he pleaded with us, but we would not listen. That is why this anguish has come upon us." ¶22 Then Reuben answered them, "Did I not tell you not to wrong the boy? But you would not listen. So now there comes a reckoning for his blood." ¶23 They did not know that Joseph understood them, since he spoke with them through an interpreter. ¶24 He turned away from them and wept; then he returned and spoke to them. And he picked out Simeon and had him bound before their eyes. ¶25 Joseph then gave orders to fill their bags with grain, to return every man's money to his sack, and to give them provisions for their journey. This was done for them. ¶26 They loaded their donkeys with their grain, and departed. ¶27 When one of them opened his sack to give his donkey fodder at the lodging place, he saw his money at the top of the sack. ¶28 He said to his brothers, "My money has been put back; here it is in my sack!" At this they lost heart and turned trembling to one another, saying, "What is this that God has done to us?" ¶29 When they came to their father Jacob in the land of Canaan, they told him all that had happened to them, saying, ¶30 "The man, the lord of the land, spoke harshly to us, and charged us with spying on the land. ¶31 But we said to him, 'We are honest men, we are not spies. ¶32 We are twelve brothers, sons of our father; one is no more, and the youngest is now with our father in the land of Canaan.' ¶33 Then the man, the lord of the land, said to us, 'By this I shall know that you are honest men: leave one of your brothers with me, take grain for the famine of your households, and go your way. ¶34 Bring your youngest brother to me, and I shall know that you are not spies but honest men. Then I will release your brother to you, and you may trade in the land.' " ¶35 As they were emptying their sacks, there in each one's sack was his bag of money. When they and their father saw their bundles of money, they were dismayed. ¶36 And their father Jacob said to them, "I am the one you have bereaved of children: Joseph is no more, and Simeon is no more, and now you would take Benjamin. All this has happened to me!" ¶37 Then Reuben said to his father, "You may kill my two sons if I do not bring him back to you. Put him in my hands, and I will bring him back to you." ¶38 But he said, "My son shall not go down with you, for his brother is dead, and he alone is left. If harm should come to him on the journey that you are to make, you would bring down my gray hairs with sorrow to Sheol."

43 ¶1 Now the famine was severe in the land. ¶2 And when they had eaten up the grain that they had brought from Egypt, their father said to them, "Go again, buy us a little more food." ¶3 But Judah said to him, "The man solemnly warned us, saying, 'You shall not see my face unless your brother is with you.' ¶4 If you will send our brother with

us, we will go down and buy you food; ¶5 but if you will not send him, we will not go down, for the man said to us, 'You shall not see my face, unless your brother is with you.' " ¶6 Israel said, "Why did you treat me so badly as to tell the man that you had another brother?" ¶7 They replied, "The man questioned us carefully about ourselves and our kindred, saying, 'Is your father still alive? Have you another brother?' What we told him was in answer to these questions. Could we in any way know that he would say, 'Bring your brother down'?" ¶8 Then Judah said to his father Israel, "Send the boy with me, and let us be on our way, so that we may live and not die—you and we and also our little ones. ¶9 I myself will be surety for him; you can hold me accountable for him. If I do not bring him back to you and set him before you, then let me bear the blame forever. ¶10 If we had not delayed, we would now have returned twice." ¶11 Then their father Israel said to them, "If it must be so, then do this: take some of the choice fruits of the land in your bags, and carry them down as a present to the man— a little balm and a little honey, gum, resin, pistachio nuts, and almonds. ¶12 Take double the money with you. Carry back with you the money that was returned in the top of your sacks; perhaps it was an oversight. ¶13 Take your brother also, and be on your way again to the man; ¶14 may God Almighty grant you mercy before the man, so that he may send back your other brother and Benjamin. As for me, if I am bereaved of my children, I am bereaved." ¶15 So the men took the present, and they took double the money with them, as well as Benjamin. Then they went on their way down to Egypt, and stood before Joseph. ¶16 When Joseph saw Benjamin with them, he said to the steward of his house, "Bring the men into the house, and slaughter an animal and make ready, for the men are to dine with me at noon." ¶17 The man did as Joseph said, and brought the men to Joseph's house. ¶18 Now the men were afraid because they were brought to Joseph's house, and they said, "It is because of the money, replaced in our sacks the first time, that we have been brought in, so that he may have an opportunity to fall upon us, to make slaves of us and take our donkeys." ¶19 So they went up to the steward of Joseph's house and spoke with him at the entrance to the house. ¶20 They said, "Oh, my lord, we came down the first time to buy food; ¶21 and when we came to the lodging place we opened our sacks, and there was each one's money in the top of his sack, our money in full weight. So we have brought it back with us. ¶22 Moreover we have brought down with us additional money to buy food. We do not know who put our money in our sacks." ¶23 He replied, "Rest assured, do not be afraid; your God and the God of your father must have put treasure in your sacks for you; I received your money." Then he brought Simeon out to them. ¶24 When the steward had brought the men into Joseph's house, and given them water, and they had washed their feet, and when he had given their donkeys fodder, ¶25 they made the present ready for Joseph's coming at noon, for they had heard that they would dine there. ¶26 When Joseph came home,

they brought him the present that they had carried into the house, and bowed to the ground before him. ¶27 He inquired about their welfare, and said, "Is your father well, the old man of whom you spoke? Is he still alive?" ¶28 They said, "Your servant our father is well; he is still alive." And they bowed their heads and did obeisance. ¶29 Then he looked up and saw his brother Benjamin, his mother's son, and said, "Is this your youngest brother, of whom you spoke to me? God be gracious to you, my son!" ¶30 With that, Joseph hurried out, because he was overcome with affection for his brother, and he was about to weep. So he went into a private room and wept there. ¶31 Then he washed his face and came out; and controlling himself he said, "Serve the meal." ¶32 They served him by himself, and them by themselves, and the Egyptians who ate with him by themselves, because the Egyptians could not eat with the Hebrews, for that is an abomination to the Egyptians. ¶33 When they were seated before him, the firstborn according to his birthright and the youngest according to his youth, the men looked at one another in amazement. ¶34 Portions were taken to them from Joseph's table, but Benjamin's portion was five times as much as any of theirs. So they drank and were merry with him.

44 ¶1 Then he commanded the steward of his house, "Fill the men's sacks with food, as much as they can carry, and put each man's money in the top of his sack. ¶2 Put my cup, the silver cup, in the top of the sack of

the youngest, with his money for the grain." And he did as Joseph told him. ¶3 As soon as the morning was light, the men were sent away with their donkeys. ¶4 When they had gone only a short distance from the city, Joseph said to his steward, "Go, follow after the men; and when you overtake them, say to them, 'Why have you returned evil for good? Why have you stolen my silver cup? ¶5 Is it not from this that my lord drinks? Does he not indeed use it for divination? You have done wrong in doing this.'" ¶6 When he overtook them, he repeated these words to them. ¶7 They said to him, "Why does my lord speak such words as these? Far be it from your servants that they should do such a thing! ¶8 Look, the money that we found at the top of our sacks, we brought back to you from the land of Canaan; why then would we steal silver or gold from your lord's house? ¶9 Should it be found with any one of your servants, let him die; moreover the rest of us will become my lord's slaves." ¶10 He said, "Even so; in accordance with your words, let it be: he with whom it is found shall become my slave, but the rest of you shall go free." ¶11 Then each one quickly lowered his sack to the ground, and each opened his sack. ¶12 He searched, beginning with the eldest and ending with the youngest; and the cup was found in Benjamin's sack. ¶13 At this they tore their clothes. Then each one loaded his donkey, and they returned to the city. ¶14 Judah and his brothers came to Joseph's house while he was still there; and they fell to the ground before him. ¶15 Joseph said to them, "What deed is this that you have done? Do you not know that one such as I can practice divination?" ¶16 And Judah said, "What can we say to my lord? What can we speak? How can we clear ourselves? God has found out the guilt of your servants; here we are then, my lord's slaves, both we and also the one in whose possession the cup has been found." ¶17 But he said, "Far be it from me that I should do so! Only the one in whose possession the cup was found shall be my slave; but as for you, go up in peace to your father." ¶18 Then Judah stepped up to him and said, "O my lord, let your servant please speak a word in my lord's ears, and do not be angry with your servant; for you are like Pharaoh himself. ¶19 My lord asked his servants, saying, 'Have you a father or a brother?' ¶20 And we said to my lord, 'We have a father, an old man, and a young brother, the child of his old age. His brother is dead; he alone is left of his mother's children, and his father loves him.' ¶21 Then you said to your servants, 'Bring him down to me, so that I may set my eyes on him.' ¶22 We said to my lord, 'The boy cannot leave his father, for if he should leave his father, his father would die.' ¶23 Then you said to your servants, 'Unless your youngest brother comes down with you, you shall see my face no more.' ¶24 When we went back to your servant my father we told him the words of my lord. ¶25 And when our father said, 'Go again, buy us a little food,' ¶26 we said, 'We cannot go down. Only if our youngest brother goes with us, will we go down; for we cannot see the man's face unless our youngest brother is with us.' ¶27 Then your servant my father said to us, 'You know that my wife bore me two sons; ¶28 one left me, and I said, Surely he has been torn to pieces; and I have never seen him since. ¶29 If you take this one also from me, and harm comes to him, you will bring down my gray hairs in sorrow to Sheol.' ¶30 Now therefore, when I come to your servant my father and the boy is not with us, then, as his life is bound up in the boy's life, ¶31 when he sees that the boy is not with us, he will die; and your servants will bring down the gray hairs of your servant our father with sorrow to Sheol. ¶32 For your servant became surety for the boy to my father, saying, 'If I do not bring him back to you, then I will bear the blame in the sight of my father all my life.' ¶33 Now therefore, please let your servant remain as a slave to my lord in place of the boy; and let the boy go back with his brothers. ¶34 For how can I go back to my father if the boy is not with me? I fear to see the suffering that would come upon my father."

45 ¶1 Then Joseph could no longer control himself before all those who stood by him, and he cried out, "Send everyone away from me." So no one stayed with him when Joseph made himself known to his brothers. ¶2 And he wept so loudly that the Egyptians heard it, and the household of Pharaoh heard it. ¶3 Joseph said to his brothers, "I am Joseph. Is my father still alive?" But his brothers could not answer him, so dismayed were they at his presence. ¶4 Then Joseph said to his brothers, "Come closer to me." And they came closer. He said, "I am your brother, Joseph, whom you sold into Egypt. ¶5 And now do not be distressed, or angry with yourselves, because you sold me here; for God sent me before you to preserve life. ¶6 For the famine has been in the land these two years; and there are five more years in which there will be neither plowing nor harvest. ¶7 God sent me before you to preserve for you a remnant on earth, and to keep alive for you many survivors. ¶8 So it was not you who sent me here, but God; he has made me a father to Pharaoh, and lord of all his house and ruler over all the land of Egypt. ¶9 Hurry and go up to my father and say to him, 'Thus says your son Joseph, God has made me lord of all Egypt; come down to me, do not delay. ¶10 You shall settle in the land of Goshen, and you shall be near me, you and your children and your children's children, as well as your flocks, your herds, and all that you have. ¶11 I will provide for you there— since there are five more years of famine to come—so that you and your household, and all that you have, will not come to poverty.' ¶12 And now your eyes and the eyes of my brother Benjamin see that it is my own mouth that speaks to you. ¶13 You must tell my father how greatly I am honored in Egypt, and all that you have seen. Hurry and bring my father down here." ¶14 Then he fell upon his brother Benjamin's neck and wept, while Benjamin wept upon his neck. ¶15 And he kissed all his brothers and wept upon them; and after that his brothers talked with him. ¶16 When the report was heard in Pharaoh's house, "Joseph's brothers have come," Pharaoh and his servants were pleased. ¶17 Pharaoh said to Joseph, "Say to your brothers, 'Do this: load your animals and go back to the land of Canaan. ¶18 Take your father and your households and come to me, so that I may give you the best of the

land of Egypt, and you may enjoy the fat of the land.' ¶19 You are further charged to say, 'Do this: take wagons from the land of Egypt for your little ones and for your wives, and bring your father, and come. ¶20 Give no thought to your possessions, for the best of all the land of Egypt is yours.'" ¶21 The sons of Israel did so. Joseph gave them wagons according to the instruction of Pharaoh, and he gave them provisions for the journey. ¶22 To each one of them he gave a set of garments; but to Benjamin he gave three hundred pieces of silver and five sets of garments. ¶23 To his father he sent the following: ten donkeys loaded with the good things of Egypt, and ten female donkeys loaded with grain, bread, and provision for his father on the journey. ¶24 Then he sent his brothers on their way, and as they were leaving he said to them, "Do not quarrel along the way." ¶25 So they went up out of Egypt and came to their father Jacob in the land of Canaan. ¶26 And they told him, "Joseph is still alive! He is even ruler over all the land of Egypt." He was stunned; he could not believe them. ¶27 But when they told him all the words of Joseph that he had said to them, and when he saw the wagons that Joseph had sent to carry him, the spirit of their father Jacob revived. ¶28 Israel said, "Enough! My son Joseph is still alive. I must go and see him before I die."

46 ¶1 When Israel set out on his journey with all that he had and came to Beer-sheba, he offered sacrifices to the God of his father Isaac. ¶2 God spoke to Israel in visions of the night, and said, "Jacob, Jacob." And he said, "Here I am." ¶3 Then he said, "I am God, the God of your father; do not be afraid to go down to Egypt, for I will make of you a great nation there. ¶4 I myself will go down with you to Egypt, and I will also bring you up again; and Joseph's own hand shall close your eyes." ¶5 Then Jacob set out from Beer-sheba; and the sons of Israel carried their father Jacob, their little ones, and their wives, in the wagons that Pharaoh had sent to carry him. ¶6 They also took their livestock and the goods that they had acquired in the land of Canaan, and they came into Egypt, Jacob and all his offspring with him, ¶7 his sons, and his sons' sons with him, his daughters, and his sons' daughters; all his offspring he brought with him into Egypt. ¶8 Now these are the names of the Israelites, Jacob and his offspring, who came to Egypt. Reuben, Jacob's firstborn, ¶9 and the children of Reuben: Hanoch, Pallu, Hezron, and Carmi. ¶10 The children of Simeon: Jemuel, Jamin, Ohad, Jachin, Zohar, and Shaul, the son of a Canaanite woman. ¶11 The children of Levi: Gershon, Kohath, and Merari. ¶12 The children of Judah: Er, Onan, Shelah, Perez, and Zerah (but Er and Onan died in the land of Canaan); and the children of Perez were Hezron and Hamul. ¶13 The children of Issachar: Tola, Puvah, Jashub, and Shimron. ¶14 The children of Zebulun: Sered, Elon, and Jahleel ¶15 (these are the sons of Leah, whom she bore to Jacob in Paddan-aram, together with his daughter Dinah; in all, his sons and his daughters numbered thirty-three). ¶16 The children of Gad: Ziphion, Haggi, Shuni, Ezbon, Eri, Arodi, and Areli. ¶17 The children of Asher: Imnah, Ishvah, Ishvi, Beriah, and their sister Serah. The

children of Beriah: Heber and Malchiel ¶18 (these are the children of Zilpah, whom Laban gave to his daughter Leah; and these she bore to Jacob—sixteen persons). ¶19 The children of Jacob's wife Rachel: Joseph and Benjamin. ¶20 To Joseph in the land of Egypt were born Manasseh and Ephraim, whom Asenath daughter of Potiphera, priest of On, bore to him. ¶21 The children of Benjamin: Bela, Becher, Ashbel, Gera, Naaman, Ehi, Rosh, Muppim, Huppim, and Ard ¶22 (these are the children of Rachel, who were born to Jacob—fourteen persons in all). ¶23 The children of Dan: Hashum. ¶24 The children of Naphtali: Jahzeel, Guni, Jezer, and Shillem ¶25 (these are the children of Bilhah, whom Laban gave to his daughter Rachel, and these she bore to Jacob—seven persons in all). ¶26 All the persons belonging to Jacob who came into Egypt, who were his own offspring, not including the wives of his sons, were sixty-six persons in all. ¶27 The children of Joseph, who were born to him in Egypt, were two; all the persons of the house of Jacob who came into Egypt were seventy. ¶28 Israel sent Judah ahead to Joseph to lead the way before him into Goshen. When they came to the land of Goshen, ¶29 Joseph made ready his chariot and went up to meet his father Israel in Goshen. He presented himself to him, fell on his neck, and wept on his neck a good while. ¶30 Israel said to Joseph, "I can die now, having seen for myself that you are still alive." ¶31 Joseph said to his brothers and to his father's household, "I will go up and tell Pharaoh, and will say to him, 'My brothers and my father's household, who

were in the land of Canaan, have come to me. ¶32 The men are shepherds, for they have been keepers of livestock; and they have brought their flocks, and their herds, and all that they have.' ¶33 When Pharaoh calls you, and says, 'What is your occupation?' ¶34 you shall say, 'Your servants have been keepers of livestock from our youth even until now, both we and our ancestors'—in order that you may settle in the land of Goshen, because all shepherds are abhorrent to the Egyptians."

47 ¶1 So Joseph went and told Pharaoh, "My father and my brothers, with their flocks and herds and all that they possess, have come from the land of Canaan; they are now in the land of Goshen." ¶2 From among his brothers he took five men and presented them to Pharaoh. ¶3 Pharaoh said to his brothers, "What is your occupation?" And they said to Pharaoh, "Your servants are shepherds, as our ancestors were." ¶4 They said to Pharaoh, "We have come to reside as aliens in the land; for there is no pasture for your servants' flocks because the famine is severe in the land of Canaan. Now, we ask you, let your servants settle in the land of Goshen." ¶5 Then Pharaoh said to Joseph, "Your father and your brothers have come to you. ¶6 The land of Egypt is before you; settle your father and your brothers in the best part of the land; let them live in the land of Goshen; and if you know that there are capable men among them, put them in charge of my livestock." ¶7 Then Joseph brought in his father Jacob, and presented him before Pharaoh, and

Jacob blessed Pharaoh. ¶8 Pharaoh said to Jacob, "How many are the years of your life?" ¶9 Jacob said to Pharaoh, "The years of my earthly sojourn are one hundred thirty; few and hard have been the years of my life. They do not compare with the years of the life of my ancestors during their long sojourn." ¶10 Then Jacob blessed Pharaoh, and went out from the presence of Pharaoh. ¶11 Joseph settled his father and his brothers, and granted them a holding in the land of Egypt, in the best part of the land, in the land of Rameses, as Pharaoh had instructed. ¶12 And Joseph provided his father, his brothers, and all his father's household with food, according to the number of their dependents. ¶13 Now there was no food in all the land, for the famine was very severe. The land of Egypt and the land of Canaan languished because of the famine. ¶14 Joseph collected all the money to be found in the land of Egypt and in the land of Canaan, in exchange for the grain that they bought; and Joseph brought the money into Pharaoh's house. ¶15 When the money from the land of Egypt and from the land of Canaan was spent, all the Egyptians came to Joseph, and said, "Give us food! Why should we die before your eyes? For our money is gone." ¶16 And Joseph answered, "Give me your livestock, and I will give you food in exchange for your livestock, if your money is gone." ¶17 So they brought their livestock to Joseph; and Joseph gave them food in exchange for the horses, the flocks, the herds, and the donkeys. That year he supplied them with food in exchange for all their livestock. ¶18 When that year was ended, they came to him the following year, and said to him, "We can not hide from my lord that our money is all spent; and the herds of cattle are my lord's. There is nothing left in the sight of my lord but our bodies and our lands. ¶19 Shall we die before your eyes, both we and our land? Buy us and our land in exchange for food. We with our land will become slaves to Pharaoh; just give us seed, so that we may live and not die, and that the land may not become desolate." ¶20 So Joseph bought all the land of Egypt for Pharaoh. All the Egyptians sold their fields, because the famine was severe upon them; and the land became Pharaoh's. ¶21 As for the people, he made slaves of them from one end of Egypt to the other. ¶22 Only the land of the priests he did not buy; for the priests had a fixed allowance from Pharaoh, and lived on the allowance that Pharaoh gave them; therefore they did not sell their land. ¶23 Then Joseph said to the people, "Now that I have this day bought you and your land for Pharaoh, here is seed for you; sow the land. ¶24 And at the harvests you shall give one-fifth to Pharaoh, and four-fifths shall be your own, as seed for the field and as food for yourselves and your households, and as food for your little ones." ¶25 They said, "You have saved our lives; may it please my lord, we will be slaves to Pharaoh." ¶26 So Joseph made it a statute concerning the land of Egypt, and it stands to this day, that Pharaoh should have the fifth. The land of the priests alone did not become Pharaoh's. ¶27 Thus Israel settled in the land of Egypt, in the region of Goshen; and they gained possessions in it, and were fruitful and multiplied exceedingly. ¶28 Jacob lived in the land of Egypt seventeen years; so the days of Jacob, the years of his life, were one hundred forty-seven years. ¶29 When the time of Israel's death drew near, he called his son Joseph and said to him, "If I have found favor with you, put your hand under my thigh and promise to deal loyally and truly with me. Do not bury me in Egypt. ¶30 When I lie down with my ancestors, carry me out of Egypt and bury me in their burial place." He answered, "I will do as you have said." ¶31 And he said, "Swear to me"; and he swore to him. Then Israel bowed himself on the head of his bed.

48 ¶1 After this Joseph was told, "Your father is ill." So he took with him his two sons, Manasseh and Ephraim. ¶2 When Jacob was told, "Your son Joseph has come to you," he summoned his strength and sat up in bed. ¶3 And Jacob said to Joseph, "God Almighty appeared to me at Luz in the land of Canaan, and he blessed me, ¶4 and said to me, 'I am going to make you fruitful and increase your numbers; I will make of you a company of peoples, and will give this land to your offspring after you for a perpetual holding.' ¶5 Therefore your two sons, who were born to you in the land of Egypt before I came to you in Egypt, are now mine; Ephraim and Manasseh shall be mine, just as Reuben and Simeon are. ¶6 As for the offspring born to you after them, they shall be yours. They shall be recorded under the names of their brothers with regard to their inheritance. ¶7 For when I came from Paddan, Rachel, alas, died in the land of Canaan on the way, while there was still some distance to go to Ephrath; and I buried

her there on the way to Ephrath" (that is, Bethlehem). ¶8 When Israel saw Joseph's sons, he said, "Who are these?" ¶9 Joseph said to his father, "They are my sons, whom God has given me here." And he said, "Bring them to me, please, that I may bless them." ¶10 Now the eyes of Israel were dim with age, and he could not see well. So Joseph brought them near him; and he kissed them and embraced them. ¶11 Israel said to Joseph, "I did not expect to see your face; and here God has let me see your children also." ¶12 Then Joseph removed them from his father's knees, and he bowed himself with his face to the earth. ¶13 Joseph took them both, Ephraim in his right hand toward Israel's left, and Manasseh in his left hand toward Israel's right, and brought them near him. ¶14 But Israel stretched out his right hand and laid it on the head of Ephraim, who was the younger, and his left hand on the head of Manasseh, crossing his hands, for Manasseh was the firstborn. ¶15 He blessed Joseph, and said, *"The God before whom my ancestors Abraham and Isaac walked, the God who has been my shepherd all my life to this day, ¶16 the angel who has redeemed me from all harm, bless the boys; and in them let my name be perpetuated, and the name of my ancestors Abraham and Isaac; and let them grow into a multitude on the earth."* ¶17 When Joseph saw that his father laid his right hand on the head of Ephraim, it displeased him; so he took his father's hand, to remove it from Ephraim's head to Manasseh's head. ¶18 Joseph said to his father, "Not so, my father! Since this one is the firstborn, put your right hand on his head." ¶19 But his father refused, and said, "I know, my son, I know; he also shall become a people, and he also shall be great. Nevertheless his younger brother shall be greater than he, and his offspring shall become a multitude of nations." ¶20 So he blessed them that day, saying, "By you Israel will invoke blessings, saying, 'God make you like Ephraim and like Manasseh.' " So he put Ephraim ahead of Manasseh. ¶21 Then Israel said to Joseph, "I am about to die, but God will be with you and will bring you again to the land of your ancestors. ¶22 I now give to you one portion more than to your brothers, the portion that I took from the hand of the Amorites with my sword and with my bow."

49 ¶1 Then Jacob called his sons, and said: "Gather around, that I may tell you what will happen to you in days to come. ¶2 *Assemble and hear, O sons of Jacob; listen to Israel your father.* ¶3 *Reuben, you are my firstborn, my might and the first fruits of my vigor, excelling in rank and excelling in power.* ¶4 *Unstable as water, you shall no longer excel because you went up onto your father's bed; then you defiled it—you went up onto my couch!* ¶5 *Simeon and Levi are brothers; weapons of violence are their swords.* ¶6 *May I never come into their council; may I not be joined to their company— for in their anger they killed men, and at their whim they hamstrung oxen.* ¶7 *Cursed be their anger, for it is fierce, and their wrath, for it is cruel! I will divide them in Jacob, and scatter them in Israel.* ¶8 *Judah, your brothers shall praise you; your hand shall be on the neck of your enemies; your father's sons shall bow down before you.* ¶9 *Judah is a lion's whelp; from the prey, my son, you have gone up. He*

crouches down, he stretches out like a lion, like a lioness—who dares rouse him up? ¶10 *The scepter shall not depart from Judah, nor the ruler's staff from between his feet, until tribute comes to him; and the obedience of the peoples is his.* ¶11 *Binding his foal to the vine and his donkey's colt to the choice vine, he washes his garments in wine and his robe in the blood of grapes;* ¶12 *his eyes are darker than wine, and his teeth whiter than milk.* ¶13 *Zebulun shall settle at the shore of the sea; he shall be a haven for ships, and his border shall be at Sidon.* ¶14 *Issachar is a strong donkey, lying down between the sheepfolds;* ¶15 *he saw that a resting place was good, and that the land was pleasant; so he bowed his shoulder to the burden, and became a slave at forced labor.* ¶16 *Dan shall judge his people as one of the tribes of Israel.* ¶17 *Dan shall be a snake by the roadside, a viper along the path, that bites the horse's heels so that its rider falls backward.* ¶18 *I wait for your salvation, O* LORD. ¶19 *Gad shall be raided by raiders, but he shall raid at their heels.* ¶20 *Asher's food shall be rich, and he shall provide royal delicacies.* ¶21 *Naphtali is a doe let loose that bears lovely fawns.* ¶22 *Joseph is a fruitful bough, a fruitful bough by a spring; his branches run over the wall.* ¶23 *The archers fiercely attacked him; they shot at him and pressed him hard.* ¶24 *Yet his bow remained taut, and his arms were made agile by the hands of the Mighty One of Jacob, by the name of the Shepherd, the Rock of Israel,* ¶25 *by the God of your father, who will help you, by the Almighty who will bless you with blessings of heaven above, blessings of the deep that lies beneath, blessings of the breasts and of the womb.* ¶26 *The blessings of your father are stronger than the blessings of the eternal mountains, the* bounties of the everlasting hills; may they be on the head of Joseph, on the brow of him who was set apart from his brothers. ¶27 Benjamin is a ravenous wolf, in the morning devouring the prey, and at evening dividing the spoil." ¶28 All these are the twelve tribes of Israel, and this is what their father said to them when he blessed them, blessing each one of them with a suitable blessing. ¶29 Then he charged them, saying to them, "I am about to be gathered to my people. Bury me with my ancestors— in the cave in the field of Ephron the Hittite, ¶30 in the cave in the field at Machpelah, near Mamre, in the land of Canaan, in the field that Abraham bought from Ephron the Hittite as a burial site. ¶31 There Abraham and his wife Sarah were buried; there Isaac and his wife Rebekah were buried; and there I buried Leah— ¶32 the field and the cave that is in it were purchased from the Hittites." ¶33 When Jacob ended his charge to his sons, he drew up his feet into the bed, breathed his last, and was gathered to his people.

50 ¶1 Then Joseph threw himself on his father's face and wept over him and kissed him. ¶2 Joseph commanded the physicians in his service to embalm his father. So the physicians embalmed Israel; ¶3 they spent forty days in doing this, for that is the time required for embalming. And he Egyptians wept for him seventy days. ¶4 When the days of weeping for him were past, Joseph addressed the household of Pharaoh, "If now I have found favor

with you, please speak to Pharaoh as follows: ¶5 My father made me swear an oath; he said, 'I am about to die. In the tomb that I hewed out for myself in the land of Canaan, there you shall bury me.' Now therefore let me go up, so that I may bury my father; then I will return." ¶6 Pharaoh answered, "Go up, and bury your father, as he made you swear to do." ¶7 So Joseph went up to bury his father. With him went up all the servants of Pharaoh, the elders of his household, and all the elders of the land of Egypt, ¶8 as well as all the household of Joseph, his brothers, and his father's household. Only their children, their flocks, and their herds were left in the land of Goshen. ¶9 Both chariots and charioteers went up with him. It was a very great company. ¶10 When they came to the threshing floor of Atad, which is beyond the Jordan, they held there a very great and sorrowful lamentation; and he observed a time of mourning for his father seven days. ¶11 When the Canaanite inhabitants of the land saw the mourning on the threshing floor of Atad, they said, "This is a grievous mourning on the part of the Egyptians." Therefore the place was named Abel-mizraim; it is beyond the Jordan. ¶12 Thus his sons did for him as he had instructed them. ¶13 They carried him to the land of Canaan and buried him in the cave of the field at Machpelah, the field near Mamre, which Abraham bought as a burial site from Ephron the Hittite. ¶14 After he had buried his father, Joseph returned to Egypt with his brothers and all who had gone up with him to bury his father. ¶15 Realizing that their father was dead, Joseph's brothers said, "What if

Joseph still bears a grudge against us and pays us back in full for all the wrong that we did to him?" ¶16 So they approached Joseph, saying, "Your father gave this instruction before he died, ¶17 'Say to Joseph: I beg you, forgive the crime of your brothers and the wrong they did in harming you.' Now therefore please forgive the crime of the servants of the God of your father." Joseph wept when they spoke to him. ¶18 Then his brothers also wept, fell down before him, and said, "We are here as your slaves." ¶19 But Joseph said to them, "Do not be afraid! Am I in the place of God? ¶20 Even though you intended to do harm to me, God intended it for good, in order to preserve a numerous people, as he is doing today. ¶21 So have no fear; I myself will provide for you and your little ones." In this way he reassured them, speaking kindly to them. ¶22 So Joseph remained in Egypt, he and his father's household; and Joseph lived one hundred ten years. ¶23 Joseph saw Ephraim's children of the third generation; the children of Machir son of Manasseh were also born on Joseph's knees. ¶24 Then Joseph said to his brothers, "I am about to die; but God will surely come to you, and bring you up out of this land to the land that he swore to Abraham, to Isaac, and to Jacob." ¶25 So Joseph made the Israelites swear, saying, "When God comes to you, you shall carry up my bones from here." ¶26 And Joseph died, being one hundred ten years old; he was embalmed and placed in a coffin in Egypt.

Notes

1. Isaiah 27:1; Psalm 72:9; Job 3:8; 26:13.
2. Everett Fox, *Genesis and Exodus: A New English Rendition with Commentary and Notes* (New York, 1983), p. 11.
3. Job 1:21.
4. Isaiah 34:9–15; Jeremiah 2:2; Job 38:26; Deuteronomy 32:10.
5. Fragmentary Targum on Genesis 4:8.
6. Genesis Rabbah Ecclesiastes 4:4.
7. Epic of Gilgamesh, XI:132–37.
8. Rudolf Otto, *The Idea of the Holy: An Inquiry into the Non-rational Factor in the Idea of the Divine and Its Relation to the Rational,* trans. John W. Harvey (Oxford, 1923), pp. 13–29.
9. Jean-Paul Sartre, *The Psychology of the Imagination* (London, 1972).
10. The different sources give different versions of the events. E believed that Ishmael was banished from the family as a baby. P, however, knew a tradition which saw him living in Abraham's household until adolescence. J (in Chapter 16) believed that Hagar had run away from Sarah's cruelty and had a revelation in the desert *before* Ishmael's birth.
11. See, for example, Genesis 20:5–6 in the NRSV, where *tam* is translated "innocence."
12. Everett Fox, *Genesis and Exodus,* p. 139.
13. 2 Samuel 19:11; Esther 4:14.
14. 2 Samuel 16:21–22.

Suggestions for Further Reading

Alter, Robert. *The Art of Biblical Narrative*. New York, 1981.

Alter, Robert, and Frank Kermode, eds. *The Literary Guide to the Bible*. Cambridge, Mass., and London, 1987.

Auerbach, Erich. *Mimesis*. New York, 1957.

Cassuto, Umberto. *A Commentary on the Book of Genesis*. 2 vols. Jerusalem, 1972, 1974.

Damrosch, David. *The Narrative Covenant*. New York, 1987.

De Vaux, Roland. *Ancient Israel*. New York and London, 1967.

Fishbane, Michael. *Text and Texture*. New York, 1979.

Fokkelman, J. P. *Narrative Art in Genesis*. Assen and Amsterdam, 1975.

Ginzberg, Louis. *The Legends of the Jews*. Philadelphia, 1933.

Gros, Louis, R. R. Kenneth, and James S. Ackerman. *More Literary Interpretations of Biblical Narratives*. Nashville, 1982.

Gros, Louis, R. R. Kenneth, James S. Ackerman, and Thayer Warshaw. *Literary Interpretations of Biblical Narratives*. Nashville, 1974.

Hendel, Ronald. *The Epic of the Patriarch: The Jacob Cycle and the Narrative Traditions of Canaan and Israel*. Atlanta, 1987.

Josipovici, Gabriel. *The Book of God: A Response to the Bible*. New Haven and London, 1988.

Levenson, Jon D. *Creation and the Persistence of Evil*. New York, 1985.

Pederson, Johannes. *Israel, Its Life and Culture*. 2 vols. Oxford and Copenhagen, 1926.

Sternberg, Meir. *The Poetics of Biblical Narrative*. Bloomington, 1985.

Vawter, Bruce. *On Genesis: A New Reading*. New York, 1977

Williams, James G. *Women Recounted: Narrative Thinking and the God of Israel*. Sheffield, 1982.

Acknowledgments

My thanks to Jane Garrett, my editor, to Peter Ginsberg and Felicity Bryan, my agents, and to Joelle Delbourgo, who gave much encouragement in the early stages. Thanks also to Katherine Hourigan, Knopf's managing editor; Melvin Rosenthal, production editor; Ted Johnson, copy editor; Anthea Lingeman, designer; and Claire Bradley, production manager. As always they did a marvelous job, even though they were up against a tight deadline.

I am also grateful to Bill Moyers for inviting me to take part in *Genesis: A Living Conversation* for PBS; this encouraged me to look again at the text and rediscover its riches. I learned much from my discussions with Michael Epstein, and from Byron E. Calame, Father Alexander Di Lella, Carol Gilligan, Blu Greenberg, Samuel D. Proctor, and Rabbi Burton L. Visotzky, who shared their insights with me so generously in our conversation on Noah and the Flood.

Index

A Note About the Author

Karen Armstrong spent seven years as a Roman Catholic nun. After leaving her order in 1969 she took a B.Litt. at Oxford, taught modern literature at the University of London, and headed the English department of a public girls' school. In 1982 she became a freelance writer and broadcaster. She has long been one of the foremost British commentators on religious affairs and is now well on her way to a similar status in the United States. In 1983 she worked in the Middle East on a six-part documentary television series on the life and works of St. Paul. Her other television work has included *Varieties of Religious Experience* (1984) and *Tongues of Fire* (1985); the latter resulted in an anthology by that name on religious and poetic expression. In 1996 she participated in Bill Moyers's television series *Genesis*. She teaches at the Leo Baeck College for the Study of Judaism and the Training of Rabbis and Teachers and is also an honorary member of the Association of Muslim Social Sciences. Her published works include *Through the Narrow Gate* (1987), *Beginning the World* (1983), *The Gospel According to Woman* (1987), *Holy War: The Crusades and Their Impact on Today's World* (1991), *The English Mystics of the Fourteenth Century* (1991), *Muhammad: A Biography of the Prophet* (1992), *A History of God: The 4000-Year Quest of Judaism, Christianity and Islam* (1993), and *Jerusalem: One City, Three Faiths* (1996). She is also a regular contributor of reviews and articles to newspapers and journals.

A Note on the Type

This book was set in Monotype Dante, a typeface designed by Giovanni Mardersteig (1892–1977). Conceived as a private type for the Officina Bodoni in Verona, Italy, Dante was originally cut only for hand composition by Charles Malin, the famous Parisian punch cutter, between 1946 and 1952. Its first use was in an edition of Boccaccio's *Trattatello in laude di Dante* that appeared in 1954. The Monotype Corporation's version of Dante followed in 1957. Although modeled on the Aldine type used for Pietro Cardinal Bembo's treatise *De Aetna* in 1495, Dante is a thoroughly modern interpretation of the venerable face.

Composed by North Market Street Graphics,
Lancaster, Pennsylvania
Printed and bound by Quebecor Printing,
Martinsburg, West Virginia
Designed by Anthea Lingeman